# BRISTOL ROVERS
*Miscellany*

# BRISTOL ROVERS
## *Miscellany*

*Rovers Trivia,
History, Facts & Stats*

**STEPHEN BYRNE**

# BRISTOL ROVERS
## *Miscellany*

© Stephen Byrne

Stephen Byrne has asserted his rights in accordance with the Copyright, Designs and Patents Act 1988 to be identified as the author of this work.

Published By:
Pitch Publishing (Brighton) Ltd
A2 Yeoman Gate
Yeoman Way
Durrington
BN13 3QZ

Email: info@pitchpublishing.co.uk
Web: www.pitchpublishing.co.uk

First published 2010

A catalogue record for this book is available from the British Library.

10-digit ISBN: 1-9054116-9-3
13-digit ISBN: 978-1-9054116-9-6

Printed and bound in India by Replika Press Pvt. Ltd.

To Stitch, Tolly, Ophelia,
Horatio and Hatty.

# FOREWORD BY PAUL TROLLOPE

There is no club in the country quite like Bristol Rovers. The sense of community, the atmosphere at home matches, and the sense of belonging among the crowd all make the club quite unique. Every club has its quirky history and this book sets out to detail some of the more fascinating and intriguing tales from down the years.

When I joined Rovers as a midfielder in June 2004, it was the eighth league club I had had the privilege of representing. I had also enjoyed the honour of representing my country in international football on nine occasions. In addition, I had seen my father build up an impressive tally of appearances with Swindon Town, his 770 league games for the Robins constituting a league record with one club that stands to this day. Nonetheless, Rovers holds a special place in my heart for it is here at the Memorial Stadium that I have been able to build a reputation as a manager, securing promotion to League One in 2007 and enjoying trips to Wembley and the Millennium Stadium along the way. And an FA Cup run that took us to the quarter-finals in 2008.

This book details some of the achievements the club has enjoyed over the past few years, as well as those of yesteryear. In addition, though, it picks up on many of the forgotten, previously lost or downright obscure facts from years gone by. Who was the first Yorkshireman to play for Rovers? How many times have the Gas been awarded two penalties in a league fixture? How many clergymen have played for the club? Which Rovers player appeared in international football for two different countries? Which player wore three differently numbered shirts in the opening nine minutes of a game?

Every football club boasts a history and the Bristol Rovers history is littered with odd and unusual pieces of trivia. These are listed here in a pocket-sized book that is an ideal gift for anyone interested in The Pirates, the club's history and the beautiful game we all enjoy. Stephen Byrne has created a book that will be indispensable to any Rovers supporter and I am delighted to be given the opportunity to promote this publication as the club pushes forward into the next era in its history.

**Paul Trollope**

# ACKNOWLEDGEMENTS

NO historical book could be compiled without considerable help from many sources. Pitch Publishing have been supportive and efficient throughout and commissioning editor Dan Tester has smoothed every path in the publishing process. Mike Jay is the author of numerous books on Bristol Rovers and I have had the honour of co-writing two club histories with him; his support and help has proved invaluable, not least with producing obscure photographs.

Mervyn Baker is a fount of knowledge about Bristol football, whilst Jim Creasy and Mike Davage are the definitive researchers into the career details of national footballers. Keith Brookman and Alan Lacock have offered generous help with details of Rovers' history and club photographer Alan Marshall has allowed unhindered access to his wealth of pictures covering generations of Rovers players. David Woods, the Bristol City historian, has also shared freely his thorough and extensive records on late-Victorian football around the Bristol area.

I am extremely grateful to each of these people. Of course, nothing in life is possible without a loving and caring family. My wife, Stitch, who has been dragged to the occasional Rovers game over more than 20 years, is a constant source of love and support. Our children, Tolly, Ophelia, Horatio and Hatty are growing up to understand that Bristol Rovers is the only football club worth following.

# INTRODUCTION

MANY years ago, someone asked me to define being a Bristol Rovers supporter. My instinct was to say that it was losing 2-1 away from home on a damp, Tuesday night; there seemed to be too many memories of games at places like Kidderminster, Lincoln and Tranmere. However, there is no place for pessimism. Being a Rovers supporter is so much more than that. I remember stirring victories in derby games; I remember glorious FA Cup wins; trips to the Millennium Stadium and Wembley; gaining promotion and the feeling of ecstasy that comes with that; and walking into a football ground, any ground, any Saturday, and the sense of expectation as the match is about to start. This book, with all its quirky tales and odd obscure anecdotes defines for me what it is to be a Rovers supporter.

We are all blessed with a favourite football club. Anyone who is a supporter of Rovers is a supporter for life; you can never shake off the attachment. It will drive you mad at times; it will fill you with enthusiasm at times; it is a life commitment and you are part of the Rovers story. Whichever team is yours, do not let others dissuade you from following them – it is part of your heritage and part of your being.

My father Kevin took me to Eastville in November 1974 to watch a tame, mid-table goalless draw and that was that. There is no escaping it – you are Rovers for life. Whilst you follow a club, it is better to know something of the background to the team you support, so here is a selection of anecdotes, tales, sagas and tragedies, tales you can tell friends and obscure details perhaps best forgotten. Within these pages, you can find a birthday hat-trick, an own goal that won the championship, a Roman crock of gold and a South African cricketer. These snippets are the gold dust on which the good ship Bristol Rovers plies its trade.

These pages are a starting-point for the next chapter in Rovers' history. The club has never appeared in top-flight football nor in an FA Cup semi-final, yet there are so many tales to tell. Keep this book with you as Rovers move on to the next chapter in the club's history with all the accompanying stories that will undoubtedly follow.

**Stephen Byrne**

## CUP FINAL VICTORY

ROVERS won their first major cup final in April 1935 when they defeated Watford 3-2 in the Third Division (South) Cup Final at The Den. Rovers raced ahead with goals from Bobby McKay and Charlie Wipfler. After Bill Lane pulled a goal back, Irvine Harwood put Rovers 3-1 ahead and, despite Mick O'Brien's last-minute goal, held on to win the trophy. Rovers competed in the tournament between 1933/34 and 1936/37. In these four seasons they played in ten matches, winning five and losing three, scoring eighteen times and conceding fifteen. No Rovers player scored as many as three times in the tournament. The largest victory was 3-0 against Swindon Town in September 1936 and the heaviest defeat was 4-2 against Bristol City in October 1935, in which the former Rovers inside-forward Willie White scored twice. Jock McLean and Bill Pickering both represented Rovers in eight Third Division (South) Cup-ties, whilst Tom Cowan and Bert Edwards both played for the side in this competition but never in the league. George McNestry, a member of Rovers' winning side in 1935, was the only footballer in history to win this tournament with two clubs, as he also did so with Coventry City in 1936. Harold Houghton, a Rovers player from November 1935, played in an astonishing tie in January 1934, in which his Exeter City side defeated Crystal Palace 11-6; the Palace keeper, appearing in his only match for that side, was the former Rovers goalkeeper Jack Beby.

## THE FIRST PIRATE

CHRONOLOGICALLY, it would appear that the first Rovers player to be born was Bill Quick. Records are incomplete, but no other player who has appeared for Rovers seems to have been born before the summer of 1853 when William Henry Quick was born in Bedminster, the second son to Charles and Elizabeth Quick, chair-makers originally from Devon. Brought up in St. Mary Redcliffe, Quick married Frances in 1876 and they lived for many years on St. Michael's Hill with their seven children. A cabinet maker by profession, Bill Quick played just once for Rovers, appearing as a centre-half against Wotton-under-Edge in January 1888, aged 34. Rovers won that fixture 1-0, Fred Laurie scoring. At the time of his death in Bristol in the autumn of 1918, at the age of 65, he was living at 585 Stapleton Road.

## PROUD TO BE A GASHEAD

OVERLOOKING the grand, old stadium at Eastville were the gasworks which, if the wind was in the wrong direction, belched gas across the Eastville terraces on match days. When Rovers left the ground in 1986, the term 'Gas' or 'Gasheads' followed the club to Bath and back to the Memorial Stadium. Perhaps it was a term of endearment, but Rovers supporters of a certain age recall the word 'Gashead' being used by Bristol City fans during the 1980/81 season. Steve Slade recalls a City fan Andy Johnson calling him a 'Gashead' in 1980 as he waited for a bus on Redcliffe Hill. That year, as Rovers used Ashton Gate for a few home games in the aftermath of the Eastville fire, the words 'no Gasheads' were allegedly written above one of the turnstiles. The first million-pound footballer Trevor Francis had an article published in 1979 which described Eastville as the worst ground on which he had ever played on account of the smell of gas. Regulars in the Princes Bar and Wheatsheaf pubs remember the term 'Gas' being in use during the 1979/80 season. Certainly, when Rovers played at Wrexham in April 1981, the song You'll Never Get Rid Of The Gas was being sung. At the local derby in April 1986, Bristol City supporters unfurled a banner in the Muller Road End at Eastville that stated simply 'Gas Busters'. Rovers' arrival at Twerton Park in 1986 prompted a greater interest in the term 'Gashead', perhaps sparked by the coincidental proximity of gasworks to the ground in Bath too, and the song Proud To Be A Gashead reverberated around the ground in that first season. Apocryphal tales indicate the *Bristol Evening Post* first used the term in 2001. Dan Warren in *Life at the Bottom* (BBC Sport, April 14th 2003) is quoted as saying "some, like me, are born a Gashead, some have Gasheadness thrust upon them". The Harper Collins dictionary accepted the definition of 'Gashead' in February 2005 as "people dwelling north of the river Frome in Bristol, supporter of Bristol Rovers Football Club".

## BLIZZARD SWEEPS IN

DOMINIC Blizzard, who joined Rovers in July 2009, scored the fastest league goal ever registered by a Stockport County player when he fired home after fourteen seconds of their 4-1 win against Hereford United in January 2009.

## YOUNGEST ROVERS TEAM

THE youngest Rovers side to appear in a league fixture was the team that won 1-0 at Wrexham on May 10th 1979, through a David Williams goal. This match constituted the only league appearance of Palmer's career.

| | | |
|---|---|---|
| Martin Thomas........ | 28/11/1959 | 19 years 163 days |
| David Palmer........... | 10/04/1961 | 18 years 30 days |
| Phil Bater................. | 26/10/1955 | 23 years 196 days |
| Peter Aitken............. | 30/06/1954 | 24 years 314 days |
| Mike England ......... | 04/01/1961 | 18 years 126 days |
| Martin Shaw ........... | 14/09/1960 | 18 years 238 days |
| Paul Petts ................ | 27/09/1961 | 19 years 225 days |
| David Williams ....... | 11/03/1955 | 24 years 60 days |
| Steve White............. | 02/01/1959 | 20 years 128 days |
| Keith Brown............ | 28/09/1959 | 19 years 102 days |
| Gary Emmanuel ..... | 01/02/1954 | 25 years 99 days |
| Sub: Gary Mabbutt. | 23/08/1961 | 17 years 250 days |

Total age 239 years 98 days
Average age 20 years 6 days

## CELEBRITY FANS

MANY clubs have notable famous names amongst their supporters. Lord Jeffrey Archer, the author and former Member of Parliament, is a Rovers fan, having watched the club play on many occasions as a young man based in Weston-super-Mare. The dance music producer Roni Size, celebrated boxers Glen Catley and Jane Couch and the former chairman of selectors for the England cricket team, David Graveney OBE, are all said to support Rovers. Although Rod Hull produced a record for the club during the 1973/74 promotion season, he was not a follower of the club's fortunes and there is equally no evidence to support the popular view that some members of the 1980s pop group Depeche Mode are 'Gasheads', not one of them hailing from the south-west of England.

## NO GOAL FOR TEN YEARS (ALMOST)

IT was very nearly a decade since he had last scored in the Football League when Ray Warren registered a goal for Rovers against Queens Park Rangers in the autumn of 1946. Three of the players on this list were not to score for many years due to World War II holding up league football; Penrice and Walter were both transferred away from the club and scored again after rejoining. Kevin Moore scored an own goal in Rovers' favour, whilst playing for Grimsby Town in August 1980 and then scored for Rovers against Birmingham City in October 1992, after a gap of twelve years and one month. Rovers' wing-half Sam Irving, whose only league goal for Rovers came in December 1932, went over twelve years without scoring – between his goal for Bristol City at Wolverhampton Wanderers in October 1914 and one for Cardiff City at home to Sunderland in March 1927. Similarly, Bob Bloomer, also a Rovers player, scored for Chesterfield against Exeter City in March 1990 and next for Cheltenham Town against Brighton in February 2001, almost eleven years later. Lee Martin scored for Manchester United in the 1990 FA Cup Final and, after a spell with Rovers, his next goal in senior football came for Bangor City in their home defeat against Carmarthen Town in the Welsh Premier League in October 2005, over fifteen years later.

9 yrs 11 mths..... Ray Warren ...........................07/11/36 v Walsall
................................................................................2/10/46 v QPR
8 yrs 8 mths....... Wally McArthur .............. 27/08/38 v Mansfield
................................................................................26/04/47 v Port Vale
7 yrs 10 mths..... Gary Penrice.......................... 07/10/89 v Fulham
................................................................................ 23/08/97 v Carlisle
7 yrs 4 mths....... Frank Curran...................... 29/04/39 v Brighton
................................................................................ 31/08/46 v Reading
6 yrs 9 mths....... Joe Walter ...................... 11/03/22 v Gillingham
................................................................................26/12/28 v Crystal Pal

## PIRATES

AS early as 1885, Rovers were known as the Purdown Poachers. By 1927, a frequent nickname for the side was the Lilywhites, reflecting that of mighty Preston North End. Rovers adopted their distinctive quartered shirts in 1931 and soon acquired the nickname – The Pirates.

## LONGEST PIRATES

THE longest gap between a player's first and last league appearances in a Rovers shirt is just short of twenty years in the case of Ray Warren. From his Football League debut as a teenager before World War II, to captaining Rovers to the Third Division (South) championship in 1952/53, Warren served Rovers over a period of nineteen years, nine months, more than three years longer than his nearest rival. Stuart Taylor, who played in more league matches than any other Rovers player, finds himself in seventh place in this list, partly as he missed so few games through injury. Warren and McArthur both saw their careers interrupted by war, whilst Jones and Biggs were transferred away from the club at one stage. George Petherbridge was the only player for any league club to score at least one goal in each of the first sixteen post-war league seasons.

Ray Warren ............... 14/03/36 ..... 17/12/55 ...... 19 years 288 days
Wally McArthur ........ 29/04/33 ..... 30/08/49 ...... 16 years 123 days
George Petherbridge . 05/10/46 ..... 30/12/61 ........ 15 years 86 days
Bobby Jones ............... 02/11/57 ..... 28/10/72 ...... 14 years 360 days
Geoff Bradford .......... 24/09/49 ..... 21/04/64 ...... 14 years 210 days
Alfie Biggs ................. 06/02/54 ..... 16/03/68 ........ 14 years 39 days
Stuart Taylor .............. 26/04/66 ..... 11/03/80 ...... 13 years 320 days
Harold Jarman ........... 26/12/59 ..... 20/04/73 ...... 13 years 115 days
Harry Bamford .......... 31/08/46 ..... 03/09/58 ........... 12 years 3 days
Frankie Prince ........... 04/05/68 ..... 01/03/80 ...... 11 years 301 days
Jackie Pitt ................. 31/08/46 ..... 01/02/58 ...... 11 years 154 days
Ray Mabbutt ............. 04/09/57 ..... 26/12/68 ...... 11 years 114 days

## BASEBALL INTERNATIONAL

LOUIS Page, who played six times for Northampton Town against Rovers in the league between 1922 and 1925, scoring twice in the Cobblers' 5-0 win in September 1924, won seven full England caps at football and was one of four brothers who represented England at baseball.

## OLDEST GOALSCORING PIRATES

THE oldest player to score for Rovers was a Welsh-speaker, Jack Evans, the sixth and youngest child of David Evans and Elizabeth Williams of Bala; a plaque bearing his name stands on the terraced house where he grew up. His three elder brothers played for Bala Press but it was 'The Bala Bang' who made the greatest name for himself in footballing circles. A Welsh international outside-left, he was Cardiff City's first professional player and scored the first goal in a competitive fixture at Ninian Park. Evans' goal for Rovers at Bournemouth in December 1927, which makes him the club's oldest goalscorer in the Football League, was the second of three first-half equalisers in a 4-3 defeat.

1. Jack Evans ...... b. 31/01/89 ... sc. 03/12/27 ........ 38 years 360 days
2. Sam Irving ...... b. 28/08/94 ... sc. 17/12/32 ........ 38 years 110 days
3. Joe Clennell .... b. 19/02/89 ... sc. 12/02/27 ........ 37 years 358 days
4. Alan Ball ........ b. 12/05/45 ... sc. 30/04/83 ........ 37 years 353 days
5. Lance Carr ..... b. 18/02/10 ... sc. 07/04/47 .......... 37 years 50 days

## JOE PAYNE

NO collection of anecdotes regarding Rovers would be complete without an entry dedicated to Joe Payne. Born in January 1914, Payne was a reserve wing-half who was called into Luton Town's forward line during an injury crisis over Easter 1936. He responded with a league record of ten goals that stands to this day, as Rovers suffered a humiliating 12-0 defeat. He scored three times before half-time and seven more after the break, registering with three headers and seven shots. Understandably, Rovers have never before or since conceded double figures in a competitive fixture. Payne enjoyed a long career elsewhere with Chelsea and West Ham United, and won one England cap, scoring the third and sixth goals as England defeated Finland 8-0 in Helsinki in May 1937. He died in April 1975, aged sixty-one. The Kenilworth Road ground in Luton has a bar dedicated to Joe Payne, just as Walsall's Bescot Stadium has a Gilbert Alsop Stand, named after a player Rovers rejected as a schoolboy. Southampton's St. Mary's has a hospitality suite named after the former Rovers striker Mick Channon.

# TWELFTH MAN

A CHANGE in league regulations meant that, from the start of the 1965/66 season, each club could nominate a substitute per game. From the summer of 1987 this was increased to two substitutes, from 1993 to three and the figure has gone up further as years have gone by. Roy McCrohan was picked, but not used, for the first game of the season. Joe Davis replaced Ray Mabbutt in the home match with Walsall in October 1965 to become the first Rovers substitute used in the league. Brian Cash's only league appearance for Rovers, against Northampton Town in January 2005, saw him come on the pitch as a substitute and then be replaced himself. Vic Barney was the first player to make his Rovers debut as a substitute, when he replaced David Stone against Torquay United in November 1966. The first Rovers player to score after coming on as substitute was Ken Ronaldson, against Barrow in November 1968, and the first to score two goals was Graham Withey against Wigan Athletic in October 1982. Ryan Williams, against Grimsby Town in February 2005, became the first Rovers substitute to score a first-half goal. At York City in September 2003, Simon Bryant became the first Rovers substitute to be sent off. When Rovers played Walsall in February 1984 both substitutes, Paul Randall and the Saddlers' player-manager Alan Buckley, scored. The first opponent to appear as a substitute against Rovers was Tony Gregory, replacing John Regan in Shrewsbury Town's 3-2 defeat at Eastville in August 1965. The first to score was Swansea's Herbie Williams in March 1966 at Eastville. Orient's Dennis Rofe, later a Rovers manager, scored against Rovers as a substitute on his league debut. In January 2008, Colchester United's substitute Anthony Wordsworth was booked for interfering at a corner and was not brought on to the pitch during the game. During the period from 1965 to 1987, when only one substitution per club was allowed, Rovers used a Football League record 43 during the 1982/83 season.

# IT'S MEE AGAIN

FORMER Rovers inside-forward Chris Ball was sent off by referee Bert Mee of Mansfield whilst playing for Walsall against Crewe Alexandra in March 1932. Then, in March 1933, he was again dismissed playing for Walsall against Crewe Alexandra. The referee was Bert Mee!

## TENTH CHILD INTERNATIONAL

"HIS power and thrust produced many goals" is how one reporter described Jack Ball, who scored four times in 22 league matches for Rovers during the 1921/22 season. A former Sheffield United inside-forward, Ball was with Bury when he won his solitary England cap, in October 1927 against Northern Ireland; he spent the entire second half in goal following an injury to Ted Hufton. Born in September 1900 to a railway labourer, George Ball, and his wife Phoebe Stewart, Jack was the only son out of six who played professional football, playing for West Ham United and Coventry City. He died in Coventry in December 1989.

## BOOKED AFTER TWENTY SECONDS

THE earliest that Rovers have conceded a penalty was after twenty seconds of the game at home to York City in January 1997. Giving away the spot kick, Andy Tillson received a yellow card, the earliest that any Rovers player has been booked in a league game. Nigel Pepper scored from the resultant penalty. But the home crowd of 4,470 was placated by Peter Beadle's subsequent equaliser and the match finished 1-1. Dominic Blizzard received a yellow card after 26 seconds against Charlton Athletic in February 2010.

## RELEGATION

ROVERS has suffered relegation on four occasions since progressing to the Football League in 1920. In 1961/62, 1980/81 and 1992/93 Rovers dropped from the second to the third tier of English football, whilst the club dropped into the fourth tier for the first time in its history at the end of the 2000/01 season. The 1980/81 season also saw Rovers gain the fewest points (23) and score the fewest goals (34) in a league season.

## MAKING MORE MONEY

THE first time that a Rovers game was all-ticket was the local derby in March 1956. An Eastville crowd of 35,324 saw Rovers run out 3-0 winners against Bristol City. The first Rovers club lottery took place in November 1977 and the first time the club wore shirts bearing a sponsors' name was the start of the 1982/83 season, when the sponsors were Great Mills DIY.

## GOALKEEPERS ARE DIFFERENT

JESSE Whatley played in more league games than any other Rovers goalkeeper; a total of 372 matches, which included a run of 246 consecutive fixtures. Rovers' first league fixture saw the club field Harry Stansfield in goal, who always wore glasses during matches. Rovers' first substitute goalkeeper to be used was Martyn Margetson, who played the final 24 minutes at AFC Bournemouth in December 1993 following the controversial sending-off of Brian Parkin. Parkin's red card against Brighton & Hove Albion two years earlier had led to full-back Ian Alexander saving the resultant penalty from John Byrne. Steve Elliott, later a Rovers player, also saved a penalty, playing for Blackpool against Chesterfield in the 2003/04 season, after goalkeeper Phil Barnes had been sent off. In October 1887, Rovers' goalkeeper Edward Tucker missed the entire second half of the game at St. George through injury, but Rovers still won 3-2. Since then injured Rovers goalkeepers have been replaced by outfield players on fourteen occasions in the league, and in two Southern League matches and two FA Cup-ties. Similarly, opposition goalkeepers have left the field injured but, on two occasions, they never even started. For the away fixtures at Aberdare and Bournemouth in the 1923/24 season, Rovers found a full-back playing the entire match for their injury-ridden opponents, the Welsh side fielding left-half Griff James in goal and the Cherries placing full-back Edgar Saxton between the sticks. The only Rovers goalkeeper to have scored was Peter Roney, who converted a penalty away to Queens Park Rangers in a Southern League game in April 1910. Ray Cashley also achieved the feat when he was at Bristol City, from a huge goal kick against Hull City in September 1973. Rovers' youth goalkeeper Mark Brain scored in the 3-2 win against Oxford United Youth in October 1983. At the start of the 1910/11 season, two opposition goalkeepers scored against Rovers in the Southern League; Brentford's Archie Ling in their 1-0 win at Eastville followed by Northampton Town's Tommy Thorpe in their 3-2 victory.

## LANDLADY'S PIANO

DAVID Harvie – a full-back born in the Ayrshire town of Saltcoats in 1886 and who appeared for Rovers in 219 Southern League games between 1910 and 1920, scoring once, a penalty against Brighton & Hove Albion in April 1912 – left the club under a cloud after allegedly selling his landlady's piano without her permission.

## STEVE BULL'S PRECURSOR

THE great Wolves predator Steve Bull scored hatfuls of goals in the 1988/89 season as the Midlands club swept all before them, but he failed to score in the two league encounters with Rovers. By 1991, he had established a goalscoring record at Molineux surpassing the career record of 162 goals in 221 league games, a Wolves club record previously held by Bill Hartill. Born in Wolverhampton in July 1905, Hartill had left Wolverhampton Wanderers for Everton and Liverpool before representing Rovers between March 1936 and the summer of 1938. Despite playing in the infamous 12-0 defeat at Luton Town in April 1936, he had scored nineteen league goals in 36 matches for Rovers before signing for Street. Latterly a licensee in Wolverhampton, he died in Walsall in July 1980.

## BALL

ROVERS first experimented with a white ball during the Whites versus Blues pre-season trial game in August 1927. It was not considered a success because the paint soon came off! Three players called Ball have appeared for Rovers in league football. Alan Ball, a World Cup winner in 1966, scored twice in seventeen league games in 1982/83, Jack Ball, also an England international, scored four times in 22 league matches in 1921/22 and Chris Ball made fifteen scoreless appearances during the 1930/31 campaign. Six opponents called Ball have represented their clubs against Rovers in the league, whilst Joseph Ball Allon, playing for Brentford in February 1994, was the first opponent to register a league hat-trick at Twerton Park.

## KEEPING IT IN THE FAMILY

TWO pairs of brothers have appeared together in a Rovers team in league action. Cliff Britton, a future England international wing-half, played in fifty games for Rovers appearing alongside his brother in Frank's sole match for Rovers in May 1930. The Townrow brothers appeared alongside each other in six league matches during the 1930s in the half-back line. Jack, an England international, played in ten league encounters for Rovers and Frank in fifty. On a similar theme, five sets of father and sons have represented Rovers in league action; Jock and Ian Hamilton, Ray and Gary Mabbutt, John and Ian Muir, John and Paul Petts and Tony and Anthony Pulis.

## TWO MATCH BALLS?

ALTHOUGH 'Smash' and 'Grab' both scored hat-tricks as Rovers won 8-2 at Brighton & Hove Albion in December 1973, the only occasion in Rovers' league history, there have been three instances of two opponents scoring hat-tricks against Rovers in the same league fixture. In April 1922, when Rovers lost 8-1 at Swansea in a Third Division (South) fixture, Bill Brown scored three times and Jimmy Collins four. A 7-2 defeat at Shrewsbury Town in October 1962 featured three goals each from Frank Clarke and Jim McLaughlin. Finally, the demoralising 9-0 defeat at Spurs in October 1977 included three goals from Ian Moores and four from Colin Lee. Also, when Rovers lost 8-1 to Queens Park Rangers in an FA Cup tie in November 1937, both Tom Cheetham and Alf Fitzgerald scored three times.

## THREE GENERATIONS AGAINST THE GAS

FIVE sets of grandfather, father and son have played in league football against Rovers; Wally, Paul and Adam Hinshelwood; Cyril, Stuart senior and Stuart junior Beavon; George, Mike and Nicky Summerbee; Doug, Neil and Luke Webb; and Dennis, Clive and Oliver Allen – Clive's younger brother Bradley played for Rovers late in his career. Adam Hinshelwood and Stuart Beavon junior were both in the Wycombe Wanderers side that won 3-2 at the Memorial Stadium in January 2010. Four sets of father and son have scored league goals against the Gas: Don and Brian Clark for Bristol City; the two Geoff Twentymans, the younger of whom became a Rovers stalwart later in his career; Joe and Steve Livingstone; and the two Stuart Beavons.

## SEEING DOUBLE

THERE have been three occasions when a pair of twins has played against Rovers in a Football League fixture. The Fisher brothers, George and John, were in the Millwall side for both games in the 1948/49 season. Ian and Roger Morgan were then in the Queens Park Rangers team for three matches against Rovers between 1964 and 1967 and Paul and Ron Futcher played six times for Luton Town against Rovers between 1975 and 1978. Charles Hudson, who played for Rovers in the 1889/90 season, was a twin; he and his brother Frank, another brother Arthur and seven sisters, were the children of a schoolmaster at Manilla Hall School in Clifton.

## DEBUT HAT-TRICK

THERE have been three occasions when a Rovers player has scored a hat-trick on his league debut for the club. Joe Riley did so in a 4-1 win at home to Bournemouth & Boscombe Atheltic in January 1932, Jimmy McCambridge repeated the feat in a 3-0 victory over Bristol City at Ashton Gate in August 1933 and Bobby Gould also scored three times, in a 4-1 win at home to Blackburn Rovers in October 1977. Ironically, Riley also scored three goals for Bournemouth against Rovers at Dean Court in September 1936. He and Mike Channon, an England international who scored all the goals as Southampton defeated Rovers 3-0 at The Dell in February 1975, are the only two Rovers players who have also scored a league hat-trick against the club.

## UNORTHODOX

GEOFF Taylor, of all Rovers players, has enjoyed perhaps the most unorthodox and unlikely career path in football. Born in Suffolk in 1923, he played for Rovers in three league matches in the 1951/52 season when regular outside-left Josser Watling was injured. Taylor, though, had the bizarre record of having represented six different league sides in a career of only ten professional matches; he played twice each for Queens Park Rangers and Brighton & Hove Albion and in one game each for Lincoln City, Reading and Norwich City. Fluent in both French and German, Taylor then played in France and Switzerland before coaching at seven separate clubs in Germany from 1955, finishing with a four-year stint at SV Bundenbach between 1980 and 1984.

## SAVING A HAT-TRICK OF PENALTIES

HIS Rovers career was all too brief – one game against Wigan Athletic in September 2000 – but goalkeeper Matt Glennon certainly made a name for himself elsewhere. Playing for Huddersfield Town against Crewe Alexandra in February 2007, he saved three penalty kicks in one game, first from Ryan Lowe four minutes before half-time and later from Gary Roberts (79 minutes) and Julien Baudet when Roberts' kick had to be retaken. Despite his efforts, Crewe still won 2-1. Glennon was also busy at the other end of the field in March 2006, scoring with a ten-yard volley two minutes from time to earn his St. Johnstone side a 2-2 draw away to Ross County in the Scottish League.

## WARTIME FOOTBALL

DURING World War I, Rovers played a series of friendlies, many against local cadet corps. The biggest victory was 20-0 against Great Western Railway in February 1919. The most goals scored by one player in a match was eight by Bill Weston in the 12-0 win over the same opposition in December 1917. During World War II, Rovers played in seasons 1939/40 and 1945/46 only. The largest win was 7-0 against Cardiff City in January 1940, in which game Albert Iles became the only player to score four times in a game – the heaviest defeat was 5-1 at Torquay United the following month. Goalkeeper Jack Weare played in 52 games during World War Two, more than any other player, whilst Vic Lambden top-scored with 21 goals. Nobby Clarke scored a hat-trick and ended up on the losing side when Rovers lost 5-4 at home to Aldershot in September 1945. Ronnie Dix, a pre-war Rovers player, scored four times as Blackpool beat Tranmere Rovers 15-3 in February 1942 and was a Football League (North) Cup winner with Blackpool in 1943. Large numbers of Rovers players fought in the two wars of whom Jimmy Morgan was involved in the Normandy Landings, Harry Liley was at Dunkirk and Fred Chadwick was taken prisoner-of-war by the Japanese in Singapore. Four Rovers players were killed in action during the First World War. John Hardman, who played in 23 Southern League games in 1914/15, was killed in France in February 1917; Willie Gerrish, the scorer of eleven goals in 49 Southern League matches between 1905 and 1909, died in France in August 1916; Harry Phillips played in 62 Southern League games for Rovers between 1910 and 1913, scoring twice, and was killed in action in 1916; and Joe Hulme, who played four times for Rovers in the 1901/02 season, was killed in action in October 1916. Harold Stone, on Rovers' books in the 1930s, although he never played in the league, died in air combat over France in July 1941.

## LOST TO THE WINNERS

ON six occasions Rovers have been knocked out of the FA Cup by the side that eventually won the trophy. In 1921 it was Spurs, 1936 Arsenal, 1951 Newcastle United, 1972 Leeds United, 1978, after a replay, Ipswich Town, and Liverpool in 1992.

## POPULAR GAS

THE largest crowd to watch any game featuring Rovers was the 62,787 who saw the goalless FA Cup quarter-final at Newcastle in 1951. The largest attendance at any Football League game in which Rovers have played was the 49,274 at Leeds United's Elland Road in 1956, for a Second Division fixture which Rovers lost 2-1. It is believed that the estimated 40,000 Rovers supporters at Wembley to see Shrewsbury Town defeated 3-1 in May 2007 is the largest single gathering of Gasheads; that day's attendance is also the largest ever at a match that Rovers have won. The lowest league crowd that Rovers have played in front of is 1,000 on three occasions: in the 3-2 win at Merthyr Town on Boxing Day 1927; in the goalless draw at Walsall in April 1930; and in the 2-1 defeat at Torquay United in December 1933. The lowest home crowd was 1,500 against Northampton Town in January 1935. The lowest crowd at any Second Division fixture featuring any club during 1957/58 was the attendance of 5,867 to see Cardiff City entertain Rovers at Ninian Park.

| | | | |
|---|---|---|---|
| 62,787 | v Newcastle United | FA Cup | 24/02/1951 |
| 61,589 | v Shrewsbury Town | Play-off | 26/05/2007 |
| 59,175 | v Huddersfield Town | Play-off | 28/05/1995 |
| 59,025 | v Doncaster Rovers | JPT Final | 01/04/2007 |
| 55,722 | v Manchester United | FA Cup | 25/01/1964 |
| 55,294 | v Everton | FA Cup | 12/02/1969 |
| 53,317 | v Tranmere Rovers | LDC Final | 20/05/1990 |
| 49,274 | v Leeds United | Div Two | 21/04/1956 |
| 45,158 | v Aston Villa | Div Three | 03/04/1972 |

## THREE DIVISIONS

ROY Clarke played for Cardiff City in their 1-0 defeat at Eastville in Division Three (South) in March 1947 and had played in Divisions One and Two by the end of August that year. He was sold to Manchester City, who completed their promotion to the top tier of English football that summer.

## PIRATE CONSECUTIVE

JESSE Whatley holds an astonishing club record; the experienced goalkeeper played for Rovers in 246 consecutive league matches over a six-year period. This impressive run, a record for all league clubs until 1951/52, only ended in 1928 when he stepped down to allow his deputy some first-team experience. Whatley played in a total of 372 league matches for his only professional club between 1920 and 1930. The Welsh international forward Dai Ward scored in a club record eight consecutive league matches over Easter 1956; Marcus Stewart scored in eight consecutive games in all competitions over New Year 1995.

| | | |
|---|---|---|
| Jesse Whatley | 246 | August 1922–April 1928 |
| Stuart Taylor | 207 | September 1968–January 1973 |
| Ray Warren | 180 | March 1948–April 1952 |
| Lindsay Parsons | 167 | September 1970–March 1974 |
| Geoff Twentyman | 164 | December 1987–August 1991 |
| Peter Sampson | 143 | August 1950–September 1953 |
| Steve Phillips | 123 | October 2006–May 2009 |
| Jackie Pitt | 122 | May 1951–January 1954 |
| Bernard Hall | 115 | April 1963–October 1965 |
| Brian Williams | 112 | January 1983–May 1985 |
| Geoff Fox | 110 | May 1951–October 1953 |
| Ian Holloway | 105 | March 1989–May 1991 |
| Jock McLean | 102 | August 1933–February 1936 |

## FIRST BLACK PLAYER

THE first black player to represent Rovers in the Football League was Lance Carr, a South African-born outside-left, who was an ever-present in the 1946/47 season, scoring eight goals. He played in both Newport County's league fixtures against Rovers in the 1938/39 season. The first black opponent was Walter Tull, born in 1888, who scored four times for Northampton Town against Rovers in a 5-0 Southern League defeat at the County Ground in April 1912. Eddie Parris was the first black opponent in the Football League. Born in January 1911 in Chepstow to Jamaican parents, his six games for Bournemouth against Rovers between 1934 and 1937 included a goal at Eastville on Boxing Day 1935 in a game Rovers won 2-1.

## LONG-LASTING OPPONENTS

THE largest gap between a player's first and last league matches against Rovers is the 21-year span of goalkeeper Alex Ferguson. This is tame in comparison with Stanley Matthews' league record of thirty years between his games against Plymouth Argyle in 1933 and in 1963. Phil Neal played against Rovers in September 1968 and in August 1986 – 18 years 348 days being the longest gap between appearances – and has only opposed Rovers twice in league fixtures. Peter Beardsley played for Carlisle United against Rovers in December 1981 and then for Fulham against Rovers in November 1998, a gap of 16 years 323 days.

1. ...21 y. 23 d. ........Alex Ferguson ....................... 05/09/25 BR 2 Gill 0
...............................................................28/09/46 BR 0 Bris C 3
2. ...19 y. 355 d. ......Ian Callaghan ........................ 16/04/60 Liv 4 BR 0
...............................................................05/04/80 Swansea 2 BR 0
3. ...19 y. 158 d. ......Alan Wright ............... 01/04/89 BR 1 Blackpool 0
............................................................... 16/09/08 Chelt'ham T 2 BR 1
4. ...18 y. 363 d. ......Carl Muggleton .............07/11/87 BR 2 Ch'field 0
...............................................................04/11/06 BR 1 Mansfield 0
5. ...18 y. 348 d. ......Phil Neal........................... 17/09/68 No'ton 2 BR 2
............................................................... 30/08/86 BR 1 Bolton 0
6. ...18 y. 278 d. ......Chris Kamara ................ 31/01/76 BR 2 Pompey 0
...............................................................05/11/94 BR 4 Bradford 0
7. ...18 y. 257 d. ......John McDermott ......... 28/11/87 BR 4 Grimsby 2
............................................................... 12/08/06 BR 1 Grimsby 0
8. ...18 y. 138 d. ......Mick Tait........................06/12/75 Oxford 2 BR 1
............................................................... 8/04/94 Hartle 2 BR 1
9. ...18 y. 134 d. ......Kevin Wilson ................... 22/11/80 BR 1 Derby 1
............................................................... 05/04/99 BR 1 No'ton 1
10. .18 y. 110 d. ......Colin Woodthorpe.........17/10/87 BR 2 Chester 2
...............................................................04/02/06 BR 1 Bury 0

## FRENCH CONNECTION

WHEN Harry Lake retired as Rovers' trainer in June 1936 he was replaced within 24 hours by Walter Moyle. Briefly an inside-forward with Merthyr Town and Crystal Palace, Moyle was better known for his spell as manager of the French First Division side Nîmes, for the 1932/33 season.

## FOUR-GOAL OPPONENTS

PROMOTED to the forward line in an injury crisis, rookie striker Joe Payne made an instant name for himself by scoring three times before half-time and seven more thereafter. For the record, his goals came after 23, 40, 43, 49, 55, 57, 65, 76, 84 and 86 minutes. Luton Town equalled a league record victory that has since been exceeded only twice, whilst Payne's record of ten goals in one league fixture is likely to stand for many decades to come. Briggs and Evans also created club goalscoring records against Rovers.

10... Joe Payne ............... 13/04/36 ........... Luton Town 12 Rovers 0
7 ..... Tommy Briggs ........ 05/02/55 ........ Blackburn Rovers 8 Rovers 3
5 ..... Johnny Evans ......... 15/09/54 ................... Liverpool 5 Rovers 3
4 ..... Jimmy Collins ........ 15/04/22 ......... Swansea Town 8 Rovers 1
4 ..... Fred Dent .............. 05/11/27 .............. Exeter City 4 Rovers 1
4 ..... Fred Baron ............ 29/03/30 ..... Southend United 6 Rovers 0
4 ..... Billy Lake .............. 21/03/31 .......... Coventry City 5 Rovers 1
4 ..... Bill Clayson ........... 28/03/32 ........ Torquay United 8 Rovers 1
4 ..... Adrian Thorne ....... 27/08/60 ................... Brighton 6 Rovers 1
4 ..... Colin Lee .............. 22/10/77 ....................... Spurs 9 Rovers 0
4 ..... Keith Cassells ........ 31/01/87 ....... Mansfield Town 5 Rovers 0
4 ..... Guy Whittingham .. 26/12/92 .............. Portsmouth 4 Rovers 1

## ZIMBABWE

THE celebrated Liverpool and Zimbabwe keeper Bruce Grobbelaar played twice in league football against Rovers during the 1996/97 season while at Plymouth Argyle, the second in February 1997 when he was aged 39 years 131 days. Jack Weare, another goalkeeper, who played in 141 league matches for Rovers in the immediate post-war years, later emigrated to Zimbabwe and worked in a bacon factory. He died in Harare in November 1994.

## SIX INTERNATIONALS

DURING the 1932/33 season, Rovers had no fewer than six full internationals on their books, though they never played in the same side. Tommy Cook, Viv Gibbins, Sam Irving, Bobby McKay, Bill Rogers and Jack Townrow were all with the club at the same time.

# REDUCED OPPOSITION

THERE have been two occasions when three opponents have received red cards against Rovers and a further six matches when two opponents have been sent off. Larry Lloyd and Carl Heggs had previously played in Rovers' colours and were sent off on their return to their former club. On Boxing Day 2007, Luton Town were reduced to nine men after 42 minutes – and lost a third player thirteen minutes from time – yet recovered from a half-time deficit to earn an unlikely draw. The game at Swindon the previous month saw four red cards, including a substitute from each side. Four men were also sent off in the goalless draw at Gillingham in August 1998.

| | |
|---|---|
| 16/10/1982 | Larry Lloyd and Alex Cribley |
| | Rovers 4 Wigan Ath. 0 FL |
| 19/08/1995 | Carl Heggs and Steve Torpey |
| | Rovers 2 Swansea City 2 FL |
| 23/09/1995 | Martin Grainger and Jamie Bates |
| | Rovers 2 Brentford 0 FL |
| 22/08/1998 | Barry Ashby and Adrian Pennock |
| | Gillingham 0 Rovers 0 FL |
| 01/04/2002 | Abdou Sall, Gary Montgomery, Ian Foster |
| | Rovers 2 Kid. H. 1 FL |
| 24/11/2007 | Jerel Ifil and Sofiane Zaaboub |
| | Swindon Town 1 Rovers 0 FL |
| 27/11/2007 | Wayne Corden and Jabo Ibehre |
| | Rovers 3 Leyton Orient 3 FA Cup |
| 26/12/2007 | Chris Coyne, Steve Robinson, Anthony Grant |
| | Rovers 1 Luton T. 1 FL |

# WAGS

IN recent years, it has become a popular pastime in the tabloid press to chart the progress of professional footballers' wives and girlfriends (WAGs). Bobby Zamora, who played for Rovers in four substitute appearances in 1999/2000, went out with Page Three girl Nicola Tappenden, while Anwar U'ddin, who made 18 (plus one as substitute) league appearances for Rovers between 2002 and 2004 – scoring one goal – dated Page Three model Leilani Dowding.

# IT'S DERBY DAY

THE first competitive local derby between the forerunners of Bristol Rovers and City took place at the Rudgeway ground, Fishponds in September 1896, when a crowd of 3,000 saw Bristol South End defeat Eastville Rovers 2-0 in the Western League thanks to goals in each half from H. Porter and J. Ross. Prior to this, there had been a series of friendlies, the first perhaps being South End's 2-1 win against Rovers at St. John's Lane, Bedminster in September 1894. The first Football League meeting was at Ashton Gate in September 1922, when Tosh Parker's goal gave Rovers a 1-0 victory. Rovers' largest league win against City was 5-1 in December 1933, while the heaviest defeat was 5-0 at Eastville in October 1926. The largest attendance at a local derby was 39,126 at Ashton Gate for an FA Cup fifth round tie in February 1958 – Rovers won 4-3. Only two players have recorded league hat-tricks in this fixture; debutant Jimmy McCambridge for Rovers in August 1933 and Don Clark for City on Valentine's Day 1948. Bill Thomson, Jackie Pitt and Ian Alexander (twice) were all sent off for Rovers in league matches against City, as were the Robins' Ernie Peacock and Rob Edwards. Ray Warren and Harry Bamford each played for Rovers in 19 league derbies, while John Atyeo scored 12 league goals for City in the fixture – Rovers' top scorer Jimmy McCambridge scored six. Terry Cooper is the only man to have managed both sides in a derby game, whilst Peter Hooper is the only player to have scored for both sides on derby day. Gary and Kevin Mabbutt make up the only pair of brothers to have opposed each other in a Bristol derby, whilst the first missed penalty by a Rovers player in a league encounter between the clubs was by Peter Beadle in March 1997.

# THE OLDEST STRIKEFORCE

ROVERS fielded a highly experienced forward line for much of the 1926/27 season. Tommy Duncan – born in September 1897 – was the youngest of the group, George Douglas was born in August 1893, Bill Culley twelve months earlier, Joe Clennell in February 1889 and Jack Evans a month before. By the end of the season, the latter two were both 38 years old and the five-man forward line had a combined age of 172.

# EARLY CHANGES

IT is very difficult to obtain accurate timings for substitutions in the pre-internet era, but it appears very likely that the earliest any Rovers player has been substituted in a league fixture was the very first minute. Gordon Fearnley's injury against Fulham saw Bruce Bannister enter the fray after just one minute; Bannister scored the only goal of the game. Chris Solly replaced Charlton Athletic's Grant Basey after 26 seconds on February 15th 2010. In the Crewe game in 2008, when Rovers made a sixth-minute substitution, Anthony Elding replaced Calvin Zola after three minutes and 49 seconds. Millwall's Ali Fuseini came on as a fourth-minute substitute against Rovers in November 2007 and his goal, timed at seven minutes and 49 seconds, is the earliest in a Rovers game from a substitute. Amongst the earliest known substitutions made by Rovers in league matches are:

10/01/1976 .. 1 min ..... Bruce Bannister replaced Gordon Fearnley
........................................................................................ v Fulham
21/09/1991 .. 2 mins ............... Lee Archer replaced Vaughan Jones
........................................................................... v Oxford United
22/12/2007 .. 3 mins .......... Chris Carruthers replaced Joe Jacobson
............................................................................ v Leeds United
14/01/2006 .. 4 mins 7 secs John Anderson replaced Craig Hinton
......................................................................... v Cheltenham Town
28/11/1970 .. 6 mins ............... Sandy Allan replaced Carl Gilbert
........................................................................... v Torquay United
27/09/2008 .. 6 mins 59 secs .. Craig Hinton replaced Steve Elliott
............................................................................ v Crewe Alexandra
03/01/2005 .. 7 mins .............. Junior Agogo replaced Dave Savage
...................................................................... v Northampton Town

# THE LAST OUTPOST

BY dint of Plymouth Argyle's relegation to the basement division in 1995, Rovers became the last club in the league to have spent its entire career in the middle two divisions. By the arrival of the new millennium, Rovers had completed eighty years as members of the Football League without ever reaching Division One or dropping into Division Four. Eventually, though, the club was relegated to the bottom tier of league football in 2001, thus ending this unusual and bizarre claim to fame.

# PLENTY OF RED CARDS

ON a cold December night at Wigan in December 1997 Rovers made the headlines for all the wrong reasons by equalling Hereford's unwanted league record of four red cards in one league match. That game apart, there have been ten further occasions when two Rovers players have been sent off in the same fixture. At Bedminster in 1897, Rovers had two men sent off before half-time and then lost their goalkeeper Louis Johns, who was injured; with eight men on the field, the side was to hold on for an improbable 2-1 win. Trevor Challis features in three occasions when two men have been dismissed and Steve Elliott in two. Lee Jones was playing in goal for Rovers in the games against Bedminster and Yeovil where Rovers were reduced to nine men before half-time. On every occasion, except the game at York in 1974, at least one of the sent off players has been a defender. The matches against Gillingham and Swindon Town featured four red cards, the latter including one for a substitute on each side.

01/01/1897 ............................. Novello Shenton and Charlie Leese
................................................. Bedminster 1 Rovers 2 ........ WL
16/03/1974 ........................... Kenny Stephens and Bruce Bannister
................................................. York City 2 Rovers 1 ............ FL
07/08/1991 ........................... Ian Alexander and Geoff Twentyman
................................................. Bristol City 3 Rovers 2 ........ GC
02/12/1997 David Pritchard, Andy Tillson, Jason Perry, Josh Low
................................................. Wigan A. 3 BR 0 ................ FL
22/08/1998 ................................... Lee Jones and Trevor Challis
................................................. Gillingham 0 Rovers 0 ......... FL
03/10/1998 ................................... Jason Roberts and Rob Trees
................................................. Rovers 1 Bournemouth 0 ..... FL
10/10/1998 ............................. Michael Meaker and Trevor Challis
................................................. No'ton T. 3 Rovers 1 ............ FL
26/12/2000 ................................... Lewis Hogg and Trevor Challis
................................................. Rovers 2 Reading 2 ............. FL
21/12/2001 ............................. Mike Trought and Vitalijs Astafjevs
................................................. Swansea City 2 Rovers 1 ...... FL
19/10/2004 ..................................... Dave Savage and Steve Elliott
................................................. Rovers 2 Yeovil Town 2 ........ FL
24/11/2007 ................................... Richard Walker and Steve Elliott
................................................. Swindon Town 1 Rovers 0 ... FL

# SOCBY

IN May 1960, Rovers played Bristol Rugby Club at the Memorial Ground in a game of 'Socby', football played with a rugby ball. Rovers turned out in their traditional quarters, whilst Bristol wore all yellow. George Emmett and the former England footballer Arthur Milton were referees. Before a crowd of 7,000, Rovers won 3-1 after second-half goals from Geoff Bradford (2), Peter Hooper and the rugby club's team captain John Blake. A total of £450 was raised for the Friends of Frenchay Hospital, whose chairman at the time was the Rovers manager, Bert Tann. A return match was played at Eastville twelve months later, with Bert Tann as referee, aided by rugby coach Tom Mahoney and former Rovers striker Bill Roost as linesmen. Despite the heavy rain, 3,000 spectators turned up. The rugby club won 3-2, though the game was sadly overshadowed by an injury to rugby player Bert McDonald that ended his career. As well as sharing a ground, several Rovers players also excelled at rugby. Ralph Jones played for Caerau before signing for Rovers in 1947 and Christian Edwards was a Wales under-16 rugby player of great promise; he scored Rovers' try when the club lost 17-7 to Bristol Shoguns in an end-of-season game in May 2005. Vaughan Jones had trials for the Wales under-19 rugby side. Jack Havelock, who scored 11 goals for Rovers in 20 league games between 1933 and 1935, was the son of Harold Havelock, whose three England caps as a flanker had included the 28-18 defeat against Wales at Ashton Gate in 1908. Harry Wilcox (Leeds Rugby League Club) was a brother of Rovers' Freddie Wilcox, while Gordon Fearnley's father and brother both played in rugby league cup finals at Wembley, for Halifax and Bradford Northern, respectively.

# UNIVERSITY NOVELTY POOL

JAMES Harvey, a goalkeeper who had played in one league game for Rovers in 1932, appeared in court in April 1934. He was charged with obtaining £60 by false pretences from two girls he employed at his 'University Novelty Pool' in Barnsley. Born in August 1911 in Huddersfield, Harvey later played for Gillingham before working as a medical orderly in Barnsley. He had previously served for four years in the 1st Battalion of the Scots Guards, winning 23 boxing prizes in a career that included 17 knock-outs.

# OWN GOALS

NO Rovers player has conceded two own goals in a league fixture, nor has any opponent in Rovers' favour. There have been 114 own goals scored for Rovers in the Football League since 1920, scored by 112 opponents. Southend United's Anthony Grant scored for Rovers in both league fixtures of the 2009/10 season; Mansfield Town's Sandy Pate also scored two own goals for Rovers, netting in their 4-1 defeat at Eastville in January 1970 and again in Rovers' 2-1 win in March 1973. The oldest opponent to score an own goal for Rovers was Ron Burgess of Swansea Town, aged 37 years 176 days, in October 1954. The youngest, Torquay United's Phil Sandercock, was 18 years and 39 days old in March 1969. Norman Sykes scored own goals in Sunderland's favour in both games of the 1961/62 season. Phil Bater scored an own goal in both legs of a League Cup tie against Walsall in August 1977. Matt O'Mahony twice scored own goals for Reading while playing for Rovers in November 1937, and then in February 1939. Phil Roberts also scored own goals for Notts County when playing for Rovers in September 1971 and February 1974. Scott Shearer, Kevin Moore, Martin Thomas and Keith Viney, all Rovers players during their careers, each scored an own goal in Rovers' favour whilst playing against the club. The only player to score an own goal for both Bristol clubs is Tom Crilly, who scored for Bristol City whilst playing for Derby County in September 1923, and for Rovers when in Crystal Palace's colours in January 1931. Rovers' defenders conceded five own goals in the 1990/91 season, whilst Rovers benefitted from four own goals from the opposition in each of 1957/58, 1969/70, 1971/72 and 1983/84 seasons. John Hills, against Liverpool in August 1961, and Sonny Parker, against Cambridge United in December 2002, both conceded own goals on their Rovers debut.

# THE TWIN TOWERS

ROVERS have played at Wembley Stadium on three occasions. In May 1990, Rovers lost 2-1 to Tranmere Rovers in the Leyland DAF Cup Final, with Devon White scoring in front of a crowd of 48,402. In May 1995, Rovers again lost 2-1, this time to Huddersfield Town in a play-off final, with Marcus Stewart scoring before a crowd of 59,175. Finally, Rovers defeated Shrewsbury Town 3-1 in a play-off final in May 2007, with Richard Walker scoring twice, and Sammy Igoe once, in front of an attendance of 61,589.

## THE HEIGHTS OF PIRACY

FOR many years, Stuart Taylor, Rovers' dependable central defender, had his own niche in the record books as the tallest player in the club's history. He had taken the accolade from Harry Liley, who was a dominant figure in Rovers' goal in the immediate post-war years. More than that, though, at a quarter of an inch taller than Chelsea's Mickey Droy, Taylor was the tallest player operating in the league. In recent years, many clubs have employed players who are taller than six feet five inches in height, and Taylor's record at Rovers fell at the start of the 2009/2010 season when Fraser Forster was signed on loan from Newcastle United; Forster's successor Mikkel Andersen then equalled the previous long-standing record. As Forster and Andersen are both goalkeepers, Stuart Taylor is not only Rovers' record appearance maker but also the tallest man to score for Rovers in competitive football.

| | |
|---|---|
| Fraser Forster | 6ft 6ins. |
| Mikkel Andersen | 6ft 5ins. |
| Stuart Taylor | 6ft 5ins. |
| Harry Liley | 6ft 4½ins. |
| Julian Alsop | 6ft 4ins. |
| Marcus Andreasson | 6ft 4ins. |
| Peter Cawley | 6ft 4ins. |
| Christian McClean | 6ft 4ins. |
| Joe Nicholls | 6ft 4ins. |

## WINNING TWO-ONE

STRANGELY, Rovers won six consecutive league fixtures 2-1 towards the tail end of the 1989/90 Third Division championship season. The victory over Fulham on March 17th marked the start of an unorthodox run of results that was completed against Chester City on April 7th. Even more bizarrely, in three of these six games Rovers were trailing at half-time. The third game in the sequence, at home to Cardiff City, was even more bizarre as Rovers trailed 1-0 as the ninety minutes were up, only to score twice in injury time for an unlikely victory.

# LONGEVITY

THE following Rovers players are known to have lived until at least their 90th birthday:

| | | |
|---|---|---|
| Joe Walter | b. 16/08/1895 .. d. 24/05/1995 | 99 |
| Ernie Coombs | b. 21/12/1912 .. d. 01/04/2008 | 95 |
| Ivor Stallard | b. 06/03/1905 .. d. Feb 1999 | 93 |
| John Black | b. 26/05/1900 .. d. 14/12/1993 | 93 |
| Leslie Hughes | b. 02/01/1896 .. d. May 1989 | 93 |
| Joe Calvert | b. 03/02/1907 .. d. 23/12/1999 | 92 |
| James Roach | b. 12/01/1864 .. d. spring 1955 | 92 |
| Chris Russell | b. 19/06/1904 .. d. 10/12/1995 | 91 |
| Ernie Whatmore | b. 25/04/1900 .. d. 31/07/1991 | 91 |
| Bill Dodgin | b. 17/04/1909 .. d. 16/10/1999 | 90 |
| Harold Rose | b. May 1900 .. d. May/1990 | c.90 |
| Phil Taylor | b. 18/09/1917 .. still living | |

The following Rovers players are known to have died aged thirty or younger:

| | | |
|---|---|---|
| Mike Barrett | b. 12/09/1959 ... d. 14/08/1984 | 24 |
| George Warne | b. 1865 .. d. spring 1891 | 25/26 |
| John Hardman | b. 1889 .. d. Feb 1917 | 27 |
| Jack Jones | b. Oct 1874 .. d. 13/09/1903 | 28 |
| Bert Watson | b. 20/11/1908 ... d. 13/10/1939 | 30 |

# SEASONAL THREESOMES

ON two occasions, Rovers players have scored five hat-tricks in a league season. In the 1926/27 campaign, Bill Culley scored three hat-tricks and Tom Williams and Ernie Whatmore one apiece. In the 1953/54 season, Geoff Bradford scored five league hat-tricks. However, Rovers conceded a club record nine hat-tricks in 42 league games during the 1930/31 season. In both April 1922 and October 1962 Rovers let in three league hat-tricks in a calendar month. Opponents scored hat-tricks in both games against Northampton Town in 1929/30, Derby County in 1961/62 and Brentford in 1993/94.

## HAT-TRICKS

AS of early February 2010, there have been 74 hat-tricks scored in the league by Rovers players (and 91 by opponents), with Geoff Bradford leading the way with nine. He registered five league trebles during the 1953/54 season in Division Two. Rovers' oldest hat-trick scorer was Bill Culley whose three strikes against Swindon Town in April 1927 came at the age of 34 years 232 days, whilst David Mehew, at 20 years 168 days, was the youngest when he netted three times at York City's Bootham Crescent in April 1988. The fastest league hat-trick by a Rovers player was the three goals in four minutes registered by Dai Ward in the 6-1 victory over Doncaster Rovers in December 1956. On only one occasion in league football have two Rovers players scored hat-tricks in the same match, Alan Warboys and Bruce Bannister at Brighton in December 1973. On three occasions, two opponents have achieved this feat. Ian Hamilton, in Rovers' 6-3 defeat at Southend United in October 1964, scored three times and ended up on the losing side. This situation has befallen four opponents; Liverpool's Kevin Lewis in April 1961, Northampton Town's Frank Large in October 1967, Ian Wood of Oldham Athletic in May 1968 (Wood's only three goals of the season) and Brentford's Denny Mundee in January 1994. The Southend and Northampton games mentioned are the only two when a player on each side has scored a league hat-trick. Derby County's Keith Havenhand in the 1961/62 season is the only player to have scored two league hat-tricks against Rovers in the same season; he was to score just fourteen goals in his career with Derby County. Bill Clayson scored three times in the final four minutes of Rovers' 8-1 defeat at Torquay United in March 1932.

## THE FIRST YORKSHIREMAN

FOR the goalless draw against Right and Might in March 1886, Rovers used inside-right Herbert Thomas Parkinson in their side; it was to be his only game for the club. Born in Barley, Yorkshire in 1864, Parkinson was in all probability the first Yorkshireman to represent the club. Brought to Bristol through his job as a railway goods clerk, he married Eliza towards the end of 1887 and, having first settled in St. Paul's, the couple moved to Derby in search of employment in 1893. They had two sons, Walter and Herbert.

## FASTEST HAT-TRICKS

THE fastest hat-tricks by Rovers players in competitive matches have been as follows:

3 in 4 mins.... Dai Ward (77, 78, 80 mins).......... 22/12/56 v. Doncaster R..... D2
3 in 9 mins.... Vic Lambden (18, 25, 27 mins)... 19/03/48 v. Aldershot........D3S
3 in 9 mins.... Peter Beadle (30, 38, 39 mins) ..... 30/11/96 v. Bury ................. D2
3 in 11 mins.. Peter Beadle (45, 51, 56 mins) ..... 10/04/98 v. Wigan Ath....... D2
3 in 15 mins.. Phil Taylor (10, 12, 25 mins)........ 18/12/35 v. Oldh' Ath. FA Cup

The quickest hat-trick by a Rovers player from the start of a match was scored by Vic Lambden against Colchester United in April 1952; his goals were timed at one minute, eight minutes and fifteen minutes. The fastest hat-trick by an opponent was registered by Burnley's Arthur Ogden in the FA Cup at Eastville in January 1909; he scored three goals in six second-half minutes (60, 63, 66).

## TWENTY-FIFTH MINUTE

JUSTIN Channing's first three goals for Rovers came in consecutive league games in November and December 1992. Rovers had previously won only two league matches all season but, not only did Rovers win all three games, but Channing scored in the 25th minute of each fixture. First, Rovers won at Leicester City and then they defeated Luton Town and Bristol City at home. The pick of Channing's three 25th-minute goals was undeniably a 35-yard strike in the 4-0 victory over Bristol City at Twerton Park. Channing scored just three league goals that season and Rovers were relegated.

## HIDING BY THE POST

AFTER 51 minutes of Rovers' visit to Brighton for a league game in October 1995 Rovers won a goal kick. The home side's George Parris waited by the goal post as Rovers' keeper Andy Collett shaped to take the kick then tackled him as he placed the ball down. As the Rovers keeper watched on, Parris rounded him and scored a goal that was allowed to stand. Brighton won the match 2-0.

## CATASTROPHIC SCORES

NO Rovers supporter will enjoy reading a list of the club's heaviest defeats in the Football League. Rovers conceded eight second-half goals at Luton Town and six goals after the break at both Spurs and Blackburn Rovers. Joe Payne famously scored a league record ten goals in the game at Kenilworth Road in 1936, whilst Tommy Briggs scored seven times for Blackburn in 1955. Ken Wookey played for Newport County when they lost 13-0 to Newcastle United in Division Two in October 1946, the widest margin in league history, and signed for Rovers two months later, playing in 54 league matches for the club, scoring nine times.

Luton Town 12 Rovers 0........Division Three (S)........ 13/04/1936
Spurs 9 Rovers 0.....................Division Two................ 22/10/1977
Swansea Town 8 Rovers 1......Division Three (S)........ 15/04/1922
Torquay United 8 Rovers 1 ....Division Three (S)........ 28/03/1932
Blackburn Rovers 8 Rovers 3 .Division Two................ 05/02/1955

## STRAW

JOE Barratt, a Rovers inside-forward who scored four goals in 21 league matches during the 1926/27 season was reputed to have always played with a piece of straw in his mouth. He also enjoyed a long career with other clubs, winning a Third Division (South) championship medal with Southampton in 1921/22. Ray Straw – who, after the reorganisation of the Football League in 1958 had replaced the northern and southern sections with Divisions Three and Four – became the first player to appear in all six divisions, played against Rovers for Derby County in three league fixtures between 1954 and 1957.

## HOME, SWEET HOME

FROM 1883, Rovers played home fixtures on Purdown; the 1884/85 season was spent at Five Acres and the club played home games on Durdham Downs from 1886 to 1891 and 1892 to 1894, with the 1891/92 season being spent on the Schoolmasters' Cricket ground. After three years at Rudgway, 1894 to 1897, Rovers played home matches at Eastville from 1897 to 1986, at Twerton Park from 1986 to 1996 and, from 1996, at the Memorial Stadium.

# ROYALTY

A ONE-MINUTE silence was held at The Den in November 1925 prior to Rovers' goalless draw with Millwall, as Alexandra, the Queen Mother and widow of Edward VII had died the previous day. Likewise, before the 1-1 draw at Southend United in January 1936, a one-minute silence was held to the memory of King George V, and before the 3-3 draw with Orient in February 1952 there was a one-minute silence for King George VI. Thirteen months later, there was a further one-minute silence, as Queen Mary, the widow of George V, had died four days before Rovers' home victory over Bournemouth & Boscombe Athletic. In September 1997, there was a two-minute silence prior to Rovers' 1-1 draw at Bournemouth in memory of Diana, Princess of Wales, who had been killed in a car crash in Paris two days earlier. Fred Leamon, Rovers' top scorer in the first post-war league season, was working as a security guard for BBC television at the marriage of Prince Charles and Diana at St. Paul's Cathedral in August 1981, when he suffered a heart attack; he died four weeks later.

# SECRETARIES

FOLLOWING accusations of the misappropriation of club funds, Rovers' club secretary Charles Ferrari was forced to resign in October 1947. He was replaced in December 1947 by John Gummow, who was joined by an additional secretary in Ron Moules, who held the post from September 1949 until his death in March 1967. Gummow was replaced by Peter Terry, who was club secretary from December 1960 until October 1980 and who died in March 2009, aged 83. Terry's replacement was Marjorie Hall, a sister of the former Rovers centre-half Larry Lloyd. Lloyd Bell was appointed club secretary in 1985, followed by Bob Twyford in 1987 and Ian Wilson in 1994; his successor was Roger Brinsford, who was replaced in 2003 by Rod Wesson.

# OLDEST OWN-GOAL SCORERS FOR ROVERS

Ron Burgess (Swansea) ....... b. 09/04/1917 og 02/12/54... 37 yrs 176 days
Jackie Deverall (Orient)....... b. 05/05/1916 og 07/02/52... 35 yrs 278 days
Tom Crilly (Crystal Palace) b. 20/07/1895 og 17/01/31... 35 yrs 181 days

## MEMBER OF PARLIAMENT

THE only Rovers player who became a Member of Parliament was Hubert Ashton, who appeared for the club as a full-back in one league match in 1925. This solitary match was a 4-1 defeat at Reading, although he later played in five league games for Orient. Born in Calcutta in February 1898, the fourth of six sons to Hubert Shorrock Ashton and Victoria Inglis, Ashton was educated at Winchester School and Cambridge, where he won Blues for cricket, as captain, football and hockey. Two of his mother's brothers had played county cricket for Kent. He was heavily involved in local politics in Essex, where he was High Sheriff in 1943 and a county councillor from 1946. In the general election of 1950, he was elected to parliament as Conservative MP for Chelmsford, a position he held until 1964. During this time, he worked as parliamentary private secretary to the Chancellor of the Exchequer, the Lord Privy Seal and the Home Secretary. He was a Church Commissioner and Alderman of Essex. In 1959, Sir Hubert Ashton was created a Knight of the British Empire. An exceptionally talented cricketer himself, having played county cricket for Essex, as well as representing Burma, he was president of the MCC from 1948 to 1970, a period that included the South African crisis of 1960/61. His three surviving brothers, Percy, Gilbert and Claude, all played county cricket, while Claude captained England in their goalless draw with Northern Ireland in October 1925. Sir Hubert Ashton married Dorothy Gaitskell, the sister of his one-time political rival, the Labour leader Hugh Gaitskell, had two sons and two daughters, and died in South Weald in June 1979 at the age of 81.

## BRITISH JEW

WHEN Joe Jacobson made his Rovers debut at Boston United in March 2007, he became the first British Jew to appear for any club in league football since Barry Silkman had retired from the game in 1979. In the meantime, a number of international Jews had appeared in the game, but Jacobson, the first Jew to appear for Rovers, made a name for himself at the club and helped turn around a season that had proved disappointing until then. By the end of May, Rovers had appeared at both the Millennium Stadium and Wembley and had gained promotion to League One.

# A LOCAL AFFAIR

TO many supporters of a certain age, the Gloucestershire Cup was an annual fixture against the old rivals from Ashton Gate. In fact, the first final was the 1-1 draw between Clifton and Warmley in March 1888, Clifton having defeated Rovers 4-1 in an earlier round. The following season, Rovers defeated Warmley 1-0 in the final to win the trophy for the first time. By the 1907/08 season, the final had become a straightforward contest between the two remaining professional clubs in Bristol – City and Rovers. Until 1947, drawn games were replayed, then the trophy was shared until 1972 when penalty shoot-outs were introduced. All in all, Rovers won the trophy on 25 occasions, 21 of these since entering the Football League in 1920. The largest win was 3-0 in August 1988, David Mehew scoring twice and Devon White once, and the heaviest defeat a 5-0 thrashing in April 1969. City's Brian Clark, in their 3-1 win in May 1962, was the only player to score a hat-trick in the fixture. Rovers failed to score in five consecutive fixtures on two separate occasions. The highest attendance at a Gloucestershire Cup match was 20,097 at Eastville in May 1955 to see Rovers win 2-1. Two Rovers players – defenders Geoff Twentyman and Ian Alexander – were sent off in the 3-2 defeat in August 1991. Cecil Gough, Martin Boyle, Marco Carota, Lee Howells, Nigel Patterson and Mark Stevens all played for Rovers in this competition but never in the league. Sadly, Herbert Edwin Smith died of injuries sustained in a Gloucestershire Cup match against Rovers in March 1896, the Bedminster player collapsing after an accidental clash of heads with Rovers' Fred Lovett.

# FIRST PROFESSIONAL

THE first professional player to sign for the club was John McLean, an outside-right who signed in 1895 and doubled as the club groundsman in the summer months. Born in Stoke-upon-Trent in the summer of 1876, the only son of James and Elizabeth McLean, he played in 63 matches for Rovers, his 28 goals including a hat-trick against Staple Hill in December 1896. McLean moved to Worcester City in November 1898 and later played league football with Walsall, West Bromwich Albion and Preston North End until 1911. He married a Midlander, Hannah, and their daughter Ada was born in Stoke in 1895.

# TWO OWN GOALS

SINCE the inception of the Football League in 1888, a total of 25 players have had the misfortune to have conceded two own goals in one fixture. None of these has been in a game featuring Rovers, although Mansfield Town's Sandy Pate and Southend United's Anthony Grant have both scored twice for Rovers in their careers. Charlton players scored all three goals in Rovers' 2-1 win in 1929, whilst Rovers contrived to lose at both Torquay United and Stoke without any of their players being credited with a goal. Mel Charles, one own goal scorer in 1954, was the holder of 31 Welsh caps, whilst his teammate Ron Burgess, then aged 37, is the oldest opponent to concede a league own goal in Rovers' favour. In October 1889, Rovers drew 3-3 at Warmley, having led 2-0 at half-time through own goals from Gay (15 minutes) and Wilmot (35 minutes).

14/03/29 ... Charlton Ath. 1 Rovers 2 .............. Norman Smith (og)
.................................................................. Albert Langford (og)
07/03/36 ... Torquay United 2 Rovers 0 ............. Allan Murray (og)
............................................................................ Jack Preece (og)
02/10/54 ... Rovers 7 Swansea Town 0 ................. Mel Charles (og)
............................................................................ Ron Burgess (og)
28/09/57 ... Rovers 5 Notts County 2 ..... George Cruickshank (og)
..................................................................... John McGrath (og)
20/01/62 ... Stoke City 2 Rovers 0 .................... Norman Sykes (og)
.................................................................... Peter Sampson (og)
01/10/05 ... Carlisle United 1 Rovers 3 ....... Kevin Gray (og), Zigor
........................................................................... Aranalde (og)

# PLATE GLASS WINDOW

FALLING down a flight of stairs at home, the Rovers full-back Stéphane Léoni hit a plate glass door and was rushed to Frenchay Hospital by his girlfriend Alex. Luckily for the full-back, he had twenty-eight stitches inserted in the wound and was able to recover fully to regain his place in the Rovers side. The Frenchman was to appear in 27 (plus a further eleven as substitute) league matches for Rovers, his only goal coming in the FA Cup, before pursuing a footballing career that took him to Scotland and Germany before playing for several seasons in French football, ending up with AS Cannes.

## SCORING AGAINST THE PIRATES

CLAUDE Ronald Eyre, born in November 1901 in Skegby, holds the record of having scored the most league goals against Rovers by any individual player. After just one league appearance for Sheffield Wednesday, he joined Bournemouth in January 1925, playing in 302 league matches, scoring 202 goals, before retiring in 1933 to work for West Hants Water and later the Southern Electricity Board. He died in Bournemouth in August 1969. Ron Eyre's fifteen goals in fifteen league matches against Rovers included two hat-tricks. He also scored in an FA Cup tie in December 1927 and again in the December 1929 game that was abandoned with Bournemouth leading 1-0. His second goal of the game at Dean Court in December 1927 was heavily disputed as Rovers' players claimed the ball had not crossed the line. He totalled ten league hat-tricks for the Cherries, Rovers being the only club against which he completed two hat-tricks. Ted Bowen (Northampton Town), Keith Havenhand (Derby County), John McKinven (Southend United) and Peter Thorne (Stoke City) are the only other players who have twice scored a league hat-trick against Rovers.

Ron Eyre ......................... 15 ........................................Bournemouth
Ted Bowen ..................... 13 ........ Northampton Town, Bristol City
Harry Morris ................. 13 .... Brentford, Millwall, Swindon Town
John Atyeo ..................... 12 ........................................... Bristol City
Tommy Briggs ............... 12 ....... Blackburn Rovers, Grimsby Town
Joe Payne ....................... 11 ...........................................Luton Town

## HAVING TO PAY THE PENALTY

HAVING lost the prolific Rickie Lambert to Southampton, Rovers supporters might have wondered if their side could continue to score as frequently. Lambert's 29 league goals had contributed to Rovers' on-field success in 2008/09 and this figure contained a tally of five penalties. Yet, no sooner had the talismanic striker departed than Rovers were awarded two penalties against Aldershot Town in a League Cup tie and, less than two weeks later, two more in a league encounter at home to Huddersfield Town. Darryl Duffy took three of these spot kicks and Jeff Hughes the other, as Rovers scored one and missed one in each match.

## GOAL AT BOTH ENDS

FIVE Rovers players and four opponents have contrived to score for both clubs in a league match involving Rovers. The first case was that of Luton Town full-back Alf Tirrell, who scored past both goalkeepers in Rovers' inaugural league season. Vic Lambden and Geoff Twentyman both managed to score the only two goals in their respective games, whilst Cambridge players registered all seven goals in the game in February 1992. The most recent example, Byron Anthony, scored for both sides in the space of three first-half minutes, his goals interspersed by a penalty successfully converted by Rovers' Richard Walker.

Alf Tirrell (Luton Town)...... 01/01/21 ....... Rovers 2 Luton Town 1
John Hamilton (Rovers)....... 08/02/30 Rovers 2 Newport County 3
Vic Lambden (Rovers) ......... 05/04/52 ............. Brighton 1 Rovers 1
Alan Waddle (Swans City)... 26/12/79 ......... Rovers 4 Swans City 1
Tim Parkin (Rovers)............. 06/03/82 ... Swindon Town 5 Rovers 2
Geoff Twentyman (Rovers).. 02/03/88 ..... Rovers 1 Notts County 1
Neil Heaney (Camb United) 28/02/92 ..... Camb United 6 Rovers 1
Graham Potter (York City) .. 22/09/01 ............ Rovers 2 York City 2
Byron Anthony (Rovers) ...... 01/09/07 ......Rovers 2 Nottm Forest 2

## ANYONE FOR TENNIS?

JACKIE Storer, who played in one league game for Rovers at Watford in September 1931, entered several top lawn tennis tournaments and won £200 in prize money from athletics. Trevor Rhodes, once a Wimbledon junior finalist, played in two league games for Rovers during the 1968/69 season. Ashley Griffiths, a Rovers midfielder in the early 1980s, won several major youth tennis tournaments in his native South Wales before turning to professional football. The former Rovers striker Robin Stubbs represented Devon at the national over-45s doubles tennis championships held at Queen's Club. Rovers' full-back Bill Pickering, who played in 217 league games for the club, later represented Accrington at inter-league table tennis.

## SHORTEST OPPONENTS

FOR two seasons, Thames Association played in Division Three (South). One of their side was Frederick John Sidney Le May, who appeared against Rovers in Thames' 4-0 defeat at Eastville in December 1930 and in the return fixture in London the following April, which Rovers won 2-1. Le May, who was born in Bethnal Green in February 1907 and died in Suffolk in September 1988, also played for Watford and Orient, though never against Rovers; he was exactly five feet tall. At seven stone, ten pounds, Le May was also Rovers' lightest opponent. The shortest opponent to score against Rovers was Steve Spriggs who, at 5ft 2ins. scored in Cambridge United's 4-1 win at the Abbey Stadium in September 1979. Sammy Brooks, half an inch taller, scored for Southend United at Eastville in February 1925. Dave Boylan, a full 5ft 3ins, scored in Grimsby Town's win against Rovers in February 1968 and John Smith, who scored a wartime goal for Plymouth Argyle against Rovers in January 1940, was also 5ft 2ins tall.

Fred Le May ....... 5ft ............................................. Thames, 1930/31
Jackie Crawford ... 5ft 2ins. ...................................... QPR, 1934/35
Steve Spriggs ....... 5ft 2ins. ................. Cambridge United, 1978/81
Sammy Brooks .... 5ft 2½ins. ................ Southend United, 1924/25
Fanny Walden ..... 5ft 2½ins. ............ Northampton Town, 1926/27

## MICHAEL OWEN

WHILST Michael Owen has never played for, or against, Rovers in competitive football, two of his relatives have. His father Terry was a professional with Bradford City and was in the Bantams' side that crashed 7-1 at Eastville in September 1971 after conceding five goals in the opening 25 minutes. Terry's five children included Michael, and Lesley who married Richie Partridge. Michael's brother-in-law joined Rovers on loan from Liverpool in the spring of 2001 and his four league appearances (plus two as substitute) and one goal were not enough to prevent the Pirates' relegation to the basement division; he went on to play for Coventry City, Sheffield Wednesday, Rotherham United, Chester City and MK Dons.

## ALF HOMER

Rovers appointed their first manager in 1899. The man selected was Alf Homer, who had been part of the coaching staff at Aston Villa, FA Cup winners and league champions in 1897. Alfred George Homer was born in Aston in 1870, the second child of Alfred Homer and his wife Sarah Ann Hinde, both Birmingham-born. His maternal grandmother, Ann Hinde, with whom he lived for a while, was a greengrocer initially from Middlesex. Alfred senior ran a brass foundry and young Alf escaped the works to be Rovers' manager from 1899 to 1920; Rovers' accession to the Football League that year saw him step down to become club secretary, a position he held until 1928. The Gloucestershire representative to the Football Association for six years from 1931, Alf Homer died in Bristol in 1937 at the age of 66.

## GENEROUS TESTIMONIAL

ROVERS' defenders were unduly generous at Frankie Prince's testimonial match in November 1978. Bristol City were the visitors to Eastville and they returned home with a 2-0 win through own goals from Rovers' centre-backs, Graham Day and Stuart Taylor. Rarely can the old rivals from across the city have been so surprised at Rovers' wonderful generosity.

## THE FIRST STEPS

IT is well documented that Rovers' existence stems from a meeting of young men at Collins' Restaurant on Stapleton Road in September 1883 to set up a sporting club. But where exactly did this meeting take place? Though all traces of these buildings have gone, the Eastville Restaurant, run by John Collins, stood on Queen's Parade, between J. Bond the grocer and George West, a furniture broker. John Collins is listed in the 1881 census as a 46-year-old 'refreshment house keeper', who had previously been in the army.

## COFFEE BREAK

THE first reference to coffee in the United Kingdom comes from deep in Rovers' territory. Samuel Codrington, a gentleman from Frampton Cotterell, died in 1709 and left a coffee mill amongst his possessions. This information comes from David Eastleigh's 1986 book, *Old Cooking Utensils*.

## SPOT-KICK HOME AND AWAY

SEVEN Rovers players have scored from the penalty spot in both league fixtures against the same opposition in one season and this feat has been achieved by five opponents. Len Emmanuel was the father of Gary Emmanuel, who later played in 59 (plus six as substitute) league matches for Rovers, scoring twice, between December 1978 and the summer of 1981.

| | | |
|---|---|---|
| George Dennis | Rovers v. Luton Town | 1930/31 |
| George McNestry | Rovers v. Gillingham | 1934/35 |
| Ray Warren | Rovers v. QPR | 1946/47 |
| Len Emmanuel (Newport Co) | Newport County v. Rovers | 1947/48 |
| Bruce Bannister | Rovers v. Rotherham United | 1972/73 |
| John Buchanan (Cardiff City) | Cardiff City v. Rovers | 1978/79 |
| Stewart Barrowclough | Rovers v. Orient | 1979/80 |
| Julian Dicks (West Ham) | West Ham United v. Rovers | 1992/93 |
| Tony Thorpe (Luton Town) | Luton Town v. Rovers | 1996/97 |
| Steve Robinson (Bournemouth) | Bournemouth v. Rovers | 1997/98 |
| Jamie Cureton | Rovers v. Reading | 1998/99 |
| Richard Walker | Rovers v. Stockport County | 2005/06 |

## GREAT DANE

THE first Danish-born player to appear in the Football League with Rovers was the tall goalkeeper Mikkel Andersen. Standing 6ft 5ins, he used his height well and was able to be a dominant force in the side's rearguard. Just twenty years of age when he arrived on loan at the Memorial Stadium, he had played for Akademisk Boldklub in his home town of Copenhagen, becoming the youngest goalkeeper ever to play in the top flight of Danish football before signing for Reading in January 2007. Following loan spells at Torquay, Brighton and Brentford, Andersen joined Rovers in September 2009 and his form helped propel Rovers into a commanding position near the top of League One.

## GREAT PIRATE VICTORIES

IN front of the national television cameras, Rovers destroyed Brian Clough's Brighton & Hove Albion side 8-2 at the Goldstone Ground in December 1973. Five first-half goals included a hat-trick from Bruce Bannister, whilst Alan Warboys ended up with four goals. This remains the only occasion that Rovers have scored as many as eight times in a Football League fixture. Rovers' largest win ever was the 20-0 wartime victory over Great Western Railway in February 1919, in which full-back Bill Panes scored the only three goals of his long Rovers career.

Brighton 2 ... Rovers 8 ......................... Div 3 ............................. 01/12/73
Rovers 7 ....... Brighton 0 .................... Div 3(S) ........................ 29/11/52
Rovers 7 ....... Swansea Town 0 ........... Div 2 ............................. 02/10/54
Rovers 7 ....... Shrewsbury Town 0 ..... Div 3 ............................. 21/03/64
Rovers 7 ....... Northampton Town 1 . Div 3(S) ........................ 16/01/35
Rovers 7 ....... Aldershot 1 .................. Div 3(S) ........................ 29/03/48
Rovers 7 ....... Bradford City 1 .......... Div 3 ............................. 04/09/71
Rovers 7 ....... Bournemouth 2 ........... Div 3(S) ........................ 26/12/25
Rovers 7 ....... Middlesbrough 2 ........ Div 2 ............................. 26/11/55
Rovers 7 ....... Grimsby Town 3 ......... Div 2 ............................. 15/11/58

## WITCHCRAFT?

BACK in 1962, the Devon hypnotist Henry Blythe offered his services to prevent Rovers' relegation from Division Two to Three. He ran psychology courses at Ruskin College, Oxford and his link was that he had a teenage son on Rovers' books at that time. Rovers' manager Bert Tann turned down the offer of help – Rovers were relegated. The week in January 2004 that the former Rovers midfielder Tony Pounder left Frome Town, the Somerset club called in a white witch called Titania Hardie. They had not won all season at home, scoring only three times on their Badger Hill Ground; Pounder had played in 102 games (plus eleven times as substitute) for Rovers in the league, scoring ten times, between 1990 and 1994.

## QUICK GOALSCORING

### By Rovers

| | | |
|---|---|---|
| 3 goals in 3 mins | 18/12/82 v. Wrexham | D3 |
| 3 goals in 4 mins | 13/09/24 v. Charlton Athletic | Div 3(S) |
| 3 goals in 4 mins | 22/12/56 v. Doncaster Rovers (Ward 3) | D2 |
| 4 goals in 16 mins | 30/11/96 v. Bury (Beadle 3) | D2 |
| 4 goals in 18 mins | 01/11/52 v. Reading | Div 3(S) |
| 4 goals in 18 mins | 29/11/52 v. Brighton | Div 3(S) |
| 5 goals in 21 mins | 07/11/31 v. Gillingham | Div 3(S) |
| 6 goals in 40 mins | 29/11/52 v. Brighton | Div 3(S) |

### By opposition

| | | |
|---|---|---|
| 3 goals in 4 mins | 28/03/32 Torquay United (Clayson 3) | Div 3(S) |
| 4 goals in 9 mins | 22/10/77 Spurs | D2 |
| 6 goals in 41 mins | 05/02/55 Blackburn Rovers (Briggs 6) | D2 |
| 8 goals in 38 mins | 13/04/36 Luton Town (Payne 8) | Div 3(S) |

FIVE goals were scored in an astonishing final eleven minutes of Rovers' game at Bury's Gigg Lane on Christmas Day 1956. Bury, who had led 3-1 after 79 minutes, won 7-2. There were six goals in a 15-minute burst in the first half of Rovers' 4-3 defeat at Bournemouth in December 1927 and six goals in 16 minutes during Rovers' 4-3 win at home to Bury in November 1996. Rovers effectively conceded two goals in 38 seconds in January 1998; the Auto Windscreens Shield tie at Walsall was lost to a Golden Goal. In the next league game, at Gillingham, Rovers conceded a goal after just 38 seconds. Lee Bulman, making his league debut for Wycombe Wanderers against Rovers in August 1998 scored just 26 seconds after coming on to the pitch, for a last-minute equaliser in a 1-1 draw. Rovers scored six goals in only ten second-half minutes in the 15-1 FA Cup win against Weymouth in November 1900. Nationally, Stockport County scored eight goals in 16 minutes against Halifax Town in January 1934.

# LEAGUE CUP TRIVIA

ROVERS played in and won the first League Cup tie ever played. The home tie against Fulham in September 1960 started at 7.15pm, whilst other games that night began at 7.30pm and, before a crowd of 20,022, Rovers won 2-1. In both 1970/71 and 1971/72, Rovers reached the fifth round, the furthest the club has ever progressed. In October 1972 Rovers won a third round replay 2-1 against Manchester United at Old Trafford. Harold Jarman has scored more League Cup goals than any other Rovers player – with nine in total – whilst Alfie Biggs scored a seasonal best of six in the 1963/64 season. The only Rovers player to score four goals in a League Cup tie was Ian Hamilton, against Shrewsbury Town in September 1963. Cardiff City's Tony Evans scored all his side's goals in the 4-4 draw at Eastville in August 1976. The 1971/72 season was the only one where Rovers were knocked out by the eventual champions – Stoke City. From 1966/67 to 1969/70, Rovers did not score in the League Cup in four consecutive seasons. Four Rovers players, Terry Cooper, Bobby Gould, Kenny Hibbitt and Ray Graydon, three of whom were to manage Rovers later in their career, also scored in a Wembley League Cup Final. Alan Hoult, Greg Taylor and Jon Beswetherick all played for Rovers in the League Cup, but never in the Football League. Graham Day, against Cardiff City in 1976, and Steve Elliott, against Norwich City in 2004, are the only two Rovers players who have been sent off in a League Cup tie.

# SMASH AND GRAB

ROVERS' Third Division promotion side of 1973/74 was spearheaded by strikers Alan Warboys ('Smash') and Bruce Bannister ('Grab'). The pair, who attained national fame during that campaign, scored 22 and 18 league goals, respectively, as Rovers returned to Division Two. In December 1973, Bannister completed a first-half hat-trick and Warboys scored four times as Rovers defeated Brighton 8-2 at the Goldstone Ground, the only time Rovers have ever scored eight goals in a league fixture. Warboys scored 53 goals in 141 league matches (plus three as substitute) for Rovers, whilst Bannister scored 80 goals in 202 league appearances (plus four as substitute). In December 1995, when Darlington won 2-1 at Scarborough in Division Three, their scorers were Gary Bannister and Gavin Worboys.

SCOTSMAN TOM STANTON PROVED AN ABLE SUPPLIER FOR GOALSCORERS SMASH AND GRAB

## AGGREGATE GOALS

THE only league match featuring Rovers that has contained as many as twelve goals was the debacle at Kenilworth Road over Easter 1936 when Joe Payne scored ten times. There have been two further matches which included eleven goals; the game at Crystal Palace in 1927 when Rovers led 3-0 only to lose 7-4, and at Blackburn in 1955, when Rovers took the lead three times before half-time only to lose to seven Tommy Briggs goals. The Football League record is seventeen goals in a match on Boxing Day 1935, when Tranmere Rovers recorded an astonishing 13-4 victory over Oldham Athletic.

12 ....... 13/04/1936.. Luton Town......................................12 v. 0 Rovers
11 ....... 16/03/1927.. Crystal Palace ......................................7 v. 4 Rovers
11 ....... 05/02/1955.. Blackburn Rovers .............................8 v. 3 Rovers
10 ....... 10/11/1934.. Rovers .......................................5 v. 5 Exeter City
10 ....... 25/12/1957.. Swansea Town ...................................6 v. 4 Rovers
10 ....... 15/11/1958.. Rovers ...................................7 v. 3 Grimsby Town
10 ....... 01/12/1973.. Brighton ..............................................2 v. 8 Rovers
10 ....... 18/11/1978.. Rovers ............................. 5 v. 5 Charlton Athletic

## OLDEST PIRATE DEBUTANTS

THE oldest player to make his league debut for Rovers was Henry Stanley Smith, a full-back with significant experience at Nottingham Forest and Darlington. He had joined Rovers as player-coach, and was to appear in only three league fixtures whilst with the club.

1. Harry Smith ...b. 11/10/08 .. pl. 16/11/46.................38 years 36 days
2. Sam Irving ......b. 28/08/94... pl. 27/08/32................37 years 364 days
3. Alan Ball .........b. 12/05/45 ... pl. 29/01/83................37 years 262 days
4. Jack Evans.......b. 31/01/89 ... pl. 28/08/26................37 years 209 days
5. Joe Clennell ....b. 19/02/89... pl. 04/09/26................37 years 197 days

# RED CARDS

THE evocatively named Novello Dunckley Shenton became the first Rovers player to be sent off when he was dismissed before half-time of the stormy Western League game at Bedminster on New Year's Day 1897. The first in the Football League was Bill Panes against Luton Town at Eastville in February 1922. Two Rovers players have been sent off on their debut for the club. Ian Weston was sent off during the FA Cup defeat at Brentford at Griffin Park in December 1986 and Wayne Carlisle received a red card at Plymouth Argyle in League Two in March 2002. Ian Alexander was sent off at Ashton Gate on three occasions; in a Gloucestershire Cup match in August 1991 and in league fixtures in September 1989 and April 1993. The earliest in a league match that Rovers have received a red card was three minutes, when Carl Saunders was sent off against West Bromwich Albion in May 1991. Robbie Ryan was dismissed after four minutes against Orient on Boxing Day 2004. The youngest Rovers player to receive a red card was Luke Basford, who was aged 17 years 87 days when he was given his marching orders against Gillingham in January 1998. Ijah Anderson was sent off in both matches against Leyton Orient in 2003/04 and Millwall's Brian Law was dismissed in both league fixtures against Rovers in 1997/98. The first time any Portsmouth player was sent off was when full-back Roderick Walker was dismissed at Fratton Park against Rovers in a Southern League encounter in January 1905.

# BERT'S ORANGES

ONCE it became known locally that he loved oranges, the hugely popular Rovers goalkeeper found his goalmouth covered in citrus fruit at home games, as the adoring home crowd warmed to a very engaging personality. Herbert Hoyle, a Yorkshireman born in Baildon in April 1920, had played for Exeter City before signing for Rovers in May 1950 for £350. Over the next three seasons, his 104 league appearances helped ease Rovers to the Third Division (South) championship in 1952/53 and he gained immense popularity on the Eastville terraces in the process. Having retired from football, he was a popular and garrulous host of the Ship Inn, at Starcross in Devon, for many years and, retiring as a publican in June 1994, died in Dawlish in July 2003 at the age of 83.

## ANGLO-SCOTTISH CUP

DESPITE two consecutive seasons in this competition, Rovers certainly enjoyed very limited success. Phil Bater, Peter Aitken and David Williams all appeared in all six games, whilst Williams was the only Rovers player to score twice. Gary Clarke played three times and scored once before making his league debut, whilst Alan Hoult, a late substitute for Paul Randall in the Cardiff City game, never appeared in the league. Tom Ritchie scored a hat-trick for Bristol City in the 1977 game and two more the following year, as Rovers' heavy defeat attracted the highest crowd at any of these games – 9,874. City went on to win in 1977/78 and again in 1979/80, with future Rovers players Donnie Gillies and Ray Cashley appearing in their side. The only other two Rovers players to win this tournament were Terry Cooper, with Middlesbrough in 1975/76, and Larry Lloyd, whilst playing for Nottingham Forest the following year.

30/07/77 ... Rovers 0 Plymouth Argyle 1 .................................................
06/08/77 ... Bristol City 3 Rovers 1 .................................... (D.Williams)
09/08/77 ... Rovers 1 Birmingham City 1 ............................ (Hamilton)
01/08/78 ... Rovers 1 Cardiff City 0 ......................................... (Randall)
05/08/78 ... Bristol City 6 Rovers 1 ............................................. (Clarke)
15/08/78 ... Fulham 2 Rovers 1 ................................... (D.Williams, pen)

## THE SHOT THAT BROKE THE NET

HARRY Barley, who scored five times in seventeen league appearances as an outside-right for Rovers in the 1935/36 season, was noted for the ferocity of his shots. One strike, when playing for New Brighton against Darlington in a Third Division (North) fixture in November 1933, was so hard that it burst the net and apparently floored a ball boy who was standing 25 yards behind the goal. Rees Williams, Merthyr Town's outside-right, equalised at Eastville in April 1921 with a shot so hard that it broke the net – the match finished 1-1. When Rovers defeated Port Vale 2-1 in December 1949, the Valiants' goal – a penalty by Stan Palk – was converted with such ferocity that it broke through the net and travelled on across the celebrated Eastville flower-beds.

# THE MYTH OF LEAD BELLY

SO, who was this songwriter Lead Belly, who wrote Goodnight Irene, Rovers' signature tune? His biography is shrouded in mystery, though he was born on a plantation near Mooringsport in Louisiana in January 1888 (perhaps 20th, 21st, 23rd or even 29th) – his gravestone says 1889 – and died in New York on December 6th 1949. A blues and folk musician, who sang about everything from women to alcohol, cattle herding to politics, and could play several instruments: "his arms were like big stove pipes, his face was powerful and he picked the twelve-string guitar" (Woody Guthrie). Huddie William Ledbetter – the son of Wesley Ledbetter, a black plantation worker, and half-Indian Sallie Brown (or perhaps Pugho) – was brought up with his step sister Australia Carr, left home at 11, and had fathered two children by Margaret Coleman before marrying Aletha Henderson, a 15-year-old, in 1908. ("I asked your mother for you – she told me that you was too young," – as one verse of Goodnight Irene goes). He later married the evocatively-named Martha Promise in 1935. Boastful, quick-tempered and proud, Lead Belly killed a relative, Will Stafford, in a fight and was sentenced in January 1918 to seven years in a Dallas prison. It was in jail both that his sobriquet originated on account of his physical toughness, and that he was 'discovered' by musicologists John and Alan Lomax in 1930, whilst Lead Belly languished in a Louisiana penitentiary on a homicide charge. Goodnight Irene was recorded in July 1933. His burgeoning music career, however, was hampered by a later sentence, between 1939 and 1940, for assault. Lead Belly started recording for Capitol Records in 1944 and set off on a European tour in 1949 only to fall ill after a few days and die on his return to the States. "The murderous old minstrel Lead Belly," (*Time* magazine, August 14th 1950), is buried in Shiloh Baptist Church cemetery back home at Mooringsport. There is some anecdotal evidence to suggest that Lead Belly's source for Goodnight Irene was the 1886 song Irene, Good Night, written by an African-American songwriter from Cincinnati, Gussie Lord Davis (1863-1899). All songs, though, need inspiration and what better source than old spirituals – "old songs, the precious music of the heart!" (William Wordsworth). Lead Belly himself claimed to have learned Goodnight Irene in 1918 from his uncle Terrell Ledbetter. Indeed, Lead Belly's premature death in 1949 meant that his fame as the self-professed 'king of all 12-string guitar players' was almost entirely posthumous.

# GOALSCORING

THE highest number of goals Rovers have scored in a Football League season is the 92 registered in the 1952/53 Third Division (South) championship season. The side scored 60 goals at home in 1951/52 and 39 away from home in 1963/64. The longest run of consecutive league matches in which Rovers scored was 26 between March and December 1927. On the other hand, Rovers scored only 34 league goals in the relegation season of 1980/81 – only 21 at home – and scored only ten league goals away from home in 1922/23. Rovers conceded a club seasonal record 95 league goals in 1935/36 and only let in 33 goals in league football in 1973/74, as well as conceding goals in a club record 36 consecutive league matches between April 1927 and February 1928. Between 1926 and 1953, Rovers conceded exactly two goals in each of nine consecutive visits to Newport County's Somerton Park. During the 1970s, Rovers avoided defeat in all 14 league matches played against Blackburn Rovers. When Middlesbrough lost 7-0 to Arsenal in January 2006, it was the first time they had conceded seven goals in a league match since their 7-2 defeat at the hands of Rovers at Eastville in November 1955. Similarly, Spurs' 9-1 win at home to Wigan Athletic in November 2009 was the first occasion they had scored as many as nine times in the league since they had defeated Rovers 9-0 at White Hart Lane in October 1977.

# A SENSE OF HUMOUR

NICK Culkin played in 45 league matches with Rovers in 2000/01, whilst on a season-long loan at the club. He certainly made his mark by displaying a sense of humour that appealed to the club's supporters. After an injury sustained at Wycombe Wanderers, in an incident involving the future Rovers striker Andy Rammell, Culkin warmed up for the next fixture with a crash helmet on. One wayward goal kick against Bristol City caused a dent in the roof of the stand. In another incident, he kicked all Swansea City's warm-up balls into the Rovers' supporters' area. In 2000, he showed his enormous appetite for the game with his enthusiastic response to Rovers' penalty shoot-out victory over Everton in the League Cup. Culkin, a former Manchester United player, sadly had to retire through injury at just 26 years old, whilst on the books of Queens Park Rangers.

# TSUNAMI

COULD it be true that a tsunami could hit Rovers' territory? Well, it is believed that one did in January 1607, when around 2,000 people died as arable lands across the Bristol area and Somerset were contaminated by salt water. The River Severn also flooded seriously in AD14 and it is possible that the St. Michael's Day Flood of September 1014 was also a tsunami. Equally, the area was affected by 'Windy Tuesday' in February 1662 when, according to Samuel Pepys, it was "too dangerous to out of doors" and over a thousand trees fell in the Forest of Dean. The 'Great Storm' of December 1703 led to a tidal surge up the River Severn, killed around 8,000 people around England and left the port of Bristol in ruins and the hinterland underwater. There was 'deep snow' in Bristol in May in both 1698 and 1767, whilst the River Frome flooded in 1720 'as high as the wall at the Ducking Stool', in 1738 causing £100,000 of damage. In November 1800, when part of Stapleton Bridge was carried away, an area of 200 acres in Eastville was flooded in March 1889 and further floods occurred in 1936, 1937, 1947 and 1968, when five inches of rain fell in Bristol on 8th and 9th July. In March 1891, heavy snow and strong easterly winds caused half a million trees to fall in England, causing 65 ships to sink and killing 220 people and 6,000 sheep.

# HOMER THE SMALLEST

BORN in Bloxwich, Staffordshire in January 1903, Syd Homer joined Rovers from Wolves in June 1927 and scored four goals in 38 league appearances before moving across the river to join Bristol City for £250 in November 1929. At just under 5ft 3ins he is narrowly the shortest player both to appear for and to score for Rovers in league action.

| | |
|---|---|
| Syd Homer | 5ft 2¾ins. |
| Joe Haverty | 5ft 3½ins. |
| Alvin Bubb | 5ft 4ins. |
| Bobby Gardiner | 5ft 4ins. |
| George Petherbridge | 5ft 4ins. |

# IT'S HALF-TIME

ROVERS have featured in only five league games where one side has scored five times before half-time. The solitary occasion when Rovers have conceded five goals before half-time came at the Vetch Field over Easter 1922 when Rovers lost 8-1 to Swansea. Since then, Rovers have scored five goals before the interval on four occasions. In the Gillingham game in 1931 – all seven goals were scored at the same end of the Eastville ground – whilst Brian Godfrey in 1971, and Bruce Bannister two years later, both registered first-half hat-tricks for the club. This compares nationally with both Tranmere Rovers and Crewe Alexandra, who have scored eight first-half goals in league fixtures. Rovers scored four first-half goals in both league fixtures against Crystal Palace in the 1926/27 season, winning 4-1 at home and losing 7-4 away. Conversely, Rovers conceded eight goals after half-time in losing 12-0 at Luton Town over Easter 1936 and six at both Blackburn Rovers in 1955 and Spurs in 1977.

15/04/22... Swansea Town (5) 8 v. Rovers (0)1
07/11/31........ Rovers (5) 5 v. Gillingham (0)2
21/03/64.. Rovers (5) 7 v. Shrewsbury Town 0
04/09/71.... Rovers (5) 7 v. Bradford City (1)1
01/12/73.............Brighton (1) 2 v. Rovers (5)8

# ANGLO-ITALIAN CUP

AS an international competition, the short-lived Anglo-Italian Cup strove to pit the wits of second-tier English clubs against their Italian counterparts. Rovers featured only in the 1992/93 season, winning once and drawing once before being eliminated on the toss of a coin. Rovers drew 2-2 with West Ham United at Upton Park, with Julian Dicks scoring twice for the Hammers and Marcus Stewart repeating the feat for Rovers. They then defeated Southend United 3-0, through a Stewart penalty and late goals from Carl Saunders and Paul Hardyman, only to lose to a coin tossed over a long-distance phone call. The former Rovers striker Devon White scored the winning goal of the 1995 final, as Notts County defeated Ascoli 2-1 at Wembley, whilst another former Rovers forward, John Rudge, was the manager of the Port Vale side that lost the 1996 final 5-2 to Genoa on the same ground.

# EASTVILLE

BACK in 1896, searching for a new ground on which to play home fixtures, Eastville Rovers bought the former Bristol Harlequins rugby ground from the Smythe family of Ashton Court. The entire 16-acre site cost Rovers only £150 and the club spent a further £1,255 in developing a modest ground into one capable of holding a 20,000 crowd. The very first match played on the ground, next to the ubiquitous gasworks, was played in April 1897 and saw Rovers take on Aston Villa and, naturally, stumble to a 5-0 defeat. For many years, flooding from the River Frome was a major issue, until a flood relief scheme was completed in 1969. The South Stand was opened in 1924, the Muller Road End developed in 1931 and the North Stand built in 1958. The floodlights were first used for the evening fixture against Ipswich Town in September 1959, which Rovers won 2-1, and for an all-time ground record crowd of 38,472 who watched Rovers draw 3-3 in the FA Cup with Preston North End four months later. In addition to football, there was greyhound racing, speedway, cricket, baseball, basketball and even American football staged at Eastville, as well as a twice-weekly market. Other uses included renting the pitch in March 1900 to a Mr Pruett for 2/6d per week to graze his horses. Following the South Stand fire in 1980, Rovers' grip on a ground they had sold in 1940 weakened and the final game played there was the 1-1 draw with Chesterfield in April 1986. Rovers' largest Football League win on the ground was 7-0 – achieved on three occasions – while there was also a 7-0 defeat at home to Grimsby Town in 1957 as well as an 8-1 FA Cup defeat against Queens Park Rangers twenty years earlier. Brighton played in 41 league games on the ground, more than any other opposition, whilst Rovers' 81 goals against Bournemouth exceed that against any other club. West Ham United remained undefeated in all eight league visits to Eastville, whilst Gillingham lost 25 of 33 games on the ground in the league. Stuart Taylor played in 275 league games on the ground, ahead of Harry Bamford (239), Harold Jarman (236), Geoff Bradford (235) and Jackie Pitt (234). Bradford's 155 league goals at Eastville, a record 24 of them coming in the 1952/53 season, surpassed Alfie Biggs (106), Harold Jarman (81) and Peter Hooper (69). Rovers played 1,279 league matches in all at Eastville, winning 693 and losing 260, scoring 2,454 goals and conceding 1,423.

## WATCHING THE GAS AT HOME

THE largest crowd at any home Rovers fixture was the 38,472 for the visit of Preston North End in an FA Cup tie in 1960 – it finished 3-3. The largest for a league game was the 35,614 for a 1-1 draw at home to Birmingham City seven years earlier. The highest crowd at any Third Division (South) game in the 1951/52 season, involving any clubs, was the 34,612 to watch Rovers defeat Bristol City 2-0 at Eastville in January 1952, with George Petherbridge and Geoff Bradford scoring the goals. The lowest home crowd for a league game was the 1,500 to see Northampton Town comprehensively beaten 7-1 in January 1935. Rovers' highest seasonal average home crowd was 24,662 in 1953/54 and the lowest 3,246 in 1986/87.

| | | | |
|---|---|---|---|
| 38,472 | v. Preston North End | FA Cup | 30/01/1960 |
| 35,972 | v. Chelsea | FA Cup | 29/01/1955 |
| 35,921 | v. Portsmouth | FA Cup | 08/01/1955 |
| 35,872 | v. Manchester United | FA Cup | 07/01/1956 |
| 35,614 | v. Birmingham City | Div Two | 17/10/1953 |
| 35,420 | v. Doncaster Rovers | FA Cup | 28/01/1956 |
| 35,420 | v. Arsenal | FA Cup | 28/01/1967 |

## CAPS WITH ROVERS

MANY players down the years have represented their country in international football before or after enjoying a spell with Rovers. However, fifteen Rovers players have also appeared in international football while on Rovers' books. Leading the way with 32 caps is Latvia's captain Vitalijs Astafjevs. Neil Slatter played ten times for Wales while at Eastville, Ronnie Maugé collected eight caps for Trinidad and Tobago, Matt O'Mahony played six times for Ireland once for Northern Ireland, Jason Roberts six times for Grenada, Marcus Browning and Nigel Pierre five times for Wales and Trinidad and Tobago respectively, whilst Ian McLean won two caps for Canada. In addition, Geoff Bradford (England), Joe Haverty (Ireland), Ronnie Briggs (Northern Ireland), Peter Hooper (Kenya) and three Welshmen, Wayne Jones, Jack Lewis and Dai Ward, won a single cap for their country while on Rovers' books.

# A TALL STORY

UP to the early 1990s, no player measuring over 6ft 6ins had plied his trade in the Football League. All that has changed and a number of statuesque players have appeared in league matches against Rovers. Of these, Futcher, Lawrence, Jones and Sako have all scored league goals against the club. Hugo Rodrigues, a Portuguese midfielder who is the tallest player to appear in the Football League, played in one fixture against Rovers for Yeovil Town at the Memorial Stadium in December 2003, which Rovers lost to a solitary goal from Nick Crittenden.

Hugo Rodrigues .......6ft 8ins.........................Yeovil Town, 2003/04
Kevin Francis............6ft 7ins............... Stockport County, 1993-95
Ian Feuer ..................6ft 7ins........................Luton Town, 1996-98
Ben Futcher..............6ft 7ins.............. Linc C, Boston U, P'boro U,
.........................................................................Grimsby T. 2002-07
Rob Jones .................6ft 7ins.................... Grimsby Town, 2004-06
Denis Lawrence........6ft 7ins ...................Wrexham, Swansea City,
.......................................................................... Crewe Alex, 2003-09
Moriko Sako.............6ft 7ins................... Torquay United, 2005/06

# PENDERGAST'S RUN

WILLIAM James Pendergast, born in North Wales in April 1915, had an undistinguished career with Rovers, scoring three goals in seven league matches between 1936, when he signed from Wolves, and his December 1937 move to non-league Colchester United. However, the final inter-war league season was a different story. Having joined Chester, he scored in thirteen consecutive league matches for the Third Division (North) side, ending the 1938/39 season as their top scorer with 26 goals in 34 league starts. He played for New Brighton in the same division after the war, his three goals against Accrington Stanley in September 1947 making him the only man in the Wirral club's history to score a hat-trick and end up on the losing side. He died in Pen-y-Groes in May 2001. His goals in thirteen consecutive league matches constitutes a Football League record that he shares with Wolverhampton Wanderers' Tom Phillipson.

## SIX GOALS BEFORE HALF-TIME

IN the Football League the highest number of goals scored before half-time is nine, when Tranmere Rovers, 8-1 ahead at the interval, beat Oldham Athletic 13-4 on Boxing Day 1935 and when Burnley – 5-4 down at half-time – lost 7-4 at home to Watford in April 2003. The highest tally in any game featuring Rovers is just six, as has happened on the ten occasions listed below.

16/03/27 ..... D3(S) .. Crystal Palace .......................... (4) 7 v. Rovers (2) 4
03/12/27 ..... D3(S) .. Bournemouth ......................... (3) 4 v. Rovers (3) 3
04/04/58 ..... D2 ....... Rovers ................................. (3) 3 v. Bristol C (3) 3
28/10/67 ..... D3 ....... Northampton Town .............. (3) 4 v. Rovers (3) 5
04/09/71 ..... D3 ....... Rovers ............................(5) 7 v. Bradford C (1) 1
01/12/73 ..... D3 ....... Brighton ................................. (1) 2 v. Rovers (5) 8
29/12/82 ..... D3 ....... Rovers ................................(4) 4 v. Exeter C (2) 4
27/09/97 ..... D2 ....... Oldham Athletic.................... (3) 4 v. Rovers (3) 4
20/12/97 ..... D2 ....... Luton Town ........................... (2) 2 v. Rovers (4) 4
09/01/99 ..... D2 ....... Rovers ................................(3) 3 v. Burnley (3) 4

## THE MAN WHO SAVED FERGIE'S JOB

IT was widely accepted that the relatively new Manchester United manager's last chance of rescuing his job would be to win the FA Cup Final replay against Crystal Palace in May 1990. Alex Ferguson's career at Old Trafford had not started well, but a solitary goal in the replay earned United the cup. The scorer, full-back Lee Martin, like his near-namesake in Palace's goal, Nigel Martyn, also played for Rovers in a career that featured just two goals, one against West Ham United in 1989 and the other the winning strike in the FA Cup Final. Martin also played for Celtic, who remained unbeaten in the first eighteen of his nineteen Scottish League appearances and in 25 league games for Rovers in the 1996/97 season. Under Ferguson's guidance, United went on to win a plethora of league and FA Cup titles as well as two Champions League finals.

## ALLEN PALMER CUP

ROVERS competed on a number of occasions in this invitation tournament. The competition was established in 1924 by Brigadier-General George Llewellyn Palmer, a former Member of Parliament for Westbury, Wiltshire, and his wife Louie Madeleine Gouldsmith, in memory of their son who had been killed in World War I. In 1927, a Joe Clennell goal earned Rovers the right to defend the cup the following year when they lost to a 20th-minute Billy McDevitt goal. The trophy was regained in 1933 through headed goals from Doug Lewis – from Ron Green's cross after 22 minutes – and George McNestry, a minute before half-time following a cross from Bobby McKay. In 1935, Rovers led 2-0 after twenty minutes, with George McNestry and Albert Taylor having scored, but were level at half-time after Fred Tully and Johnny McIlwane had replied for the Saints after Irvine Harwood gave Rovers a 50th-minute lead. Rovers dominated and Taylor and Harwood both added their second goals of the game. The following year, the match against Bournemouth & Boscombe Athletic finished goalless and Rovers scored twice in extra-time through Harold Houghton and Ted Buckley to secure victory before Meynell Burgin scored a consolation goal a minute from time. The trophy was then conceded to Bournemouth in 1937 when, despite veteran Billy Hartill's 76th-minute goal, Rovers lost to an outstanding second-half hat-trick from former player, Joe Riley.

> 07/05/1927 .................Rovers 1 Bristol City 0
> 28/04/1928 .................Exeter City 1 Rovers 0
> 03/05/1933 .... Rovers 2 Nottingham Forest 0
> 27/04/1935 ............. Rovers 5 Southampton 2
> 29/04/1935 .... Rovers 2 Bournemouth 1 (aet)
> 28/04/1937 .............Bournemouth 3 Rovers 1

## LIFE-SAVING

ROVERS' physiotherapist Roy Dolling saved the lives of two Rovers players following separate incidents. Central defender Aiden McCaffrey swallowed his tongue during the Associate Members' Cup-tie against Southend United in April 1984 and was saved by Dolling's prompt actions. During an FA Cup game with Fisher Athletic in November 1988, Dolling helped save the life of Rovers' defender Ian Alexander, who had also swallowed his tongue.

## CHRISTMAS DAY

FOR many years it was customary for clubs to play regular league fixtures on Christmas Day. Rovers played a total of 22 games on 25th December, winning eight, drawing five and losing nine. The club's final Christmas Day match was the remarkable 6-4 defeat at Swansea in 1957. The largest league win was 5-1 at home to Southend United in 1926 and the heaviest defeat the 7-2 loss at Bury in 1956. A further pattern was that clubs frequently met the same opposition home and away as a double-header on Christmas Day and Boxing Day. Nationwide, this threw up some interesting sets of results and Rovers were involved in some strange scores down the years. Most bizarrely, Rovers lost 7-2 at Bury on Christmas Day 1956 and then beat the same opposition 6-1 at home 24 hours later, with Peter Hooper scoring a hat-trick. In 1925, having lost 2-0 away, Rovers defeated Bournemouth 7-2 at home. In 1919, after losing 6-2 away, Rovers beat Fulham 4-1 at Eastville and in 1937, Rovers and Walsall both won their respective home fixtures 5-2. Having lost 6-4 at Swansea on Christmas Day 1957, Rovers defeated the same opposition 3-0 at home on Boxing Day. Rovers' goalless draw with Port Vale on Christmas Day 1950 was played at Stoke City's Victoria Ground. In 1919, Rovers played competitive fixtures on four consecutive days over the Christmas period.

## WHAT'S IN A NAME?

ARGUABLY, the most obscure name of any Rovers player down the years was that of Novello Dunckley Shenton. This young man was born in Stoke-on-Trent in the summer of 1875, the fifth of eight children born to a beer seller, David Shenton and his wife Emma who lived in Church Street in the town. Novello's siblings were a little more fortunate, his brothers being David, Albert and Oscar, while there were four sisters in Beatrice, Evelyn, Blanche and Alice. A plumber by trade, Shenton moved to Bristol and signed up with Rovers on June 15th 1896. An inside-forward and wing-half, he appeared for the club in 36 matches over two seasons, without scoring, before leaving Rovers in 1898. He was one of two Rovers players dismissed before half-time in January 1897, when Rovers also lost their goalkeeper through injury yet held on for a momentous 2-1 victory away to Bedminster.

## DANGEROUS WORLD

THOMAS Stephens, of 9 Lion Street, Easton, died in April 1891 after an accident at Proctor's Fertiliser Works, deep in Rovers territory. A labourer at the works, he and Charles Tovey were shifting manure when a log holding the undermined pile gave way. Stephens, aged 50, suffered a fractured skull and died, his body being identified by his son Frederick. William Sidney, aged thirteen, a lead smelter along with his father at Bayley & Co. of Upper Easton, died in January 1836 when an exploding boiler caused a stack of chimneys to fall. Young William was scalded and covered in bricks, dying later that day. Engineer William England also died in the same accident.

## CIVIL WAR EVACUEE

ANTONIO Gallego, who had been evacuated from the Spanish Civil War, played in just one Football League game during his career. He was Norwich City's goalkeeper in their 3-3 draw with Rovers at Eastville in March 1947.

## PRISON FOOTBALL

ROVERS are the only Football League club that has played in a match which took place in a prison. The 11-0 win against Erlestoke Prison in 1982 was watched solely by prisoners.

## TWO GOALSCORING SUBSTITUTES

THE first time that Rovers were involved in a league game in which two substitutes scored for either team was at the Abbey Stadium in Cambridge in February 1992. Both Chris Leadbitter and John Taylor scored as Cambridge United ran up a comfortable 6-1 victory in Division Two.

## SCOTTIE THE FIRST

SCOTTIE Milne of Bedminster received the first red card shown in a Rovers match, scoring his side's second goal before being dismissed for a challenge on Rovers' Claude Hodgson in a Birmingham and District League match in May 1893. Rovers won 5-2, with Hodgson scoring once and three Bills – Rogers (2), Thompson and Laurie – scoring the other goals.

# TRANSFERS

BECAUSE transfer fees were rarely made public, it is difficult to trace the highest fees paid or received for players down the years. Britain's first six-figure transfer deal was the £110,000 Everton paid for the future Rovers midfielder, Blackpool's Alan Ball in August 1966. As far as Rovers are concerned, the first £50,000 paid was for Gary Emmanuel from Birmingham City in January 1979; this figure was overtaken when Stewart Barrowclough was signed again from Birmingham City that July for £100,000. Justin Skinner cost £130,000 from Fulham in August 1991 while Andy Tillson joined from Queens Park Rangers in November 1992 for £370,000. Rovers received £55,000 from Portsmouth for Phil Roberts in May 1973, Stoke City paid £180,000 for Paul Randall over Christmas 1978 and Steve White's move to Luton Town 12 months later pulled in £195,000. Nigel Martyn became Britain's first million-pound goalkeeper when he joined Crystal Palace in November 1989. This record was broken when Palace paid £1,600,000 for striker Gareth Taylor in September 1995 and both Barry Hayles, to Fulham in November 1998, and Jason Roberts, to West Bromwich Albion in July 2000, earned Rovers £2,000,000. Jack Rutherford is believed to have become the first player in the world to be transferred by telegram. He signed for Rovers in September 1922, while in North America, and was met by Rovers' officials as he disembarked after a year overseas.

# OLDEST PIRATES IN TOWN

WHILST no player has appeared in league football after his 40th birthday, two former Rovers players have done exactly that with other clubs. The celebrated full-back Terry Cooper's last game for Bristol City was against York City in October 1984, when he was aged 40 years 86 days. Goalkeeper Joe Calvert last played for Leicester City against Southampton in December 1947, when he was aged 40 years 313 days.

1. Jack Evans ..........b. 31/01/89.... pl. 09/04/28..............39 years 69 days
2. Sam Irving .........b. 28/08/94.... pl. 22/04/33............38 years 237 days
3. Harry Bamford ..b. 08/02/20.... pl. 03/09/58............38 years 209 days
4. Harry Smith ......b. 11/10/08.... pl. 25/12/46..............38 years 75 days
5. Kenny Hibbitt ...b. 03/01/51.... pl. 11/03/89..............38 years 67 days

# TRAGEDY

VETERAN full-back Harry Bamford, who had played in 486 league games for Rovers between 1946 and 1958, was killed in a road accident in Bristol in October 1958. Manager Bert Tann said that; "a part of Bristol Rovers died with him". Mickey Barrett, a popular 24-year-old winger, died of cancer in hospital in August 1984, just as his team-mates were involved in pre-season training. Two former Rovers players died whilst competing in local football matches: Roy Davies, a Rovers player in 1928, died during a parks game in October 1944; Roy James, a Rovers player in 1961, died in April 1990. Tommy Cook, a Rovers player between 1931 and 1933, committed suicide in Brighton in January 1950. Rovers signed George Rounce in 1935 but, before the former Queens Park Rangers and Fulham player had been able to make the side, he died in October 1936 of tuberculosis, aged 31. Jack Jones, who scored six goals for Rovers against Weymouth in the FA Cup in November 1900, joined Spurs from Rovers and died in London of typhoid in September 1903, aged 28. Herbert Edward Smith, a Bedminster player, died following a clash of heads sustained in a match against Rovers in March 1896. Billy Callender, who played for Crystal Palace against Rovers, hanged himself at the age of 26 in July 1932 at the Selhurst Park ground, following the death of his fiancée.

# RISING STAR

A POPULAR figure at the Madejski Stadium, though he had scored four times there for Rovers in a match in 1999, Jamie Cureton was honoured in an unusual way in September 2002. Reading supporters named a star after him in the constellation Perseus – Right Ascension 3h 26m 20s, declination +35* 20' 25". Cureton scored 72 league goals for Rovers in 167 (plus nine as substitute) league matches between 1996 and 2000 and 50 goals in 74 (plus 34 as substitute) games in the league for the Royals before pursuing a career in South Korea. Cureton was the first opponent to score a league hat-trick at the Madejski Stadium – for Rovers in January 1999 – and also the first home player to do so – against Brentford in September 2000. He was to return to haunt Rovers again in October 2009, scoring the final goal as Rovers crashed 5-1 to Norwich City at Carrow Road.

## OLDEST OPPOSITION LINE-UP

PROBABLY the oldest side to play against Rovers in the Football League was Ipswich Town on December 18th 1948. A solitary goal from inside-forward Jimmy Morgan gave Rovers victory before a crowd of 8,751 at Portman Road.

| | | |
|---|---|---|
| Tom Brown ........born ............. 26/10/1919 ................29 years 53 days |
| Dave Bell ................................... 24/12/1909................38 years 359 days |
| George Rumbold ..................... 10/07/1911................37 years 161 days |
| George Perrett.......................... 02/05/1915................33 years 169 days |
| Harry Baird .............................. 17/08/1913................35 years 123 days |
| Jackie Brown............................. 08/11/1914...................34 years 40 days |
| John Dempsey.......................... 22/06/1913................35 years 179 days |
| Bill Jennings ............................ 07/01/1920................28 years 346 days |
| Tommy Parker.......................... 13/02/1924................24 years 309 days |
| Jackie Little............................... 17/05/1912................36 years 215 days |
| Ossie Parry................................ 16/08/1908................40 years 124 days |

Total age: 374 years 253 days
Average age: 34 years 23 days

## HESTER TILLY

IN October 1844, William Tilly, who farmed eleven acres at Ashley Down, heard that his 23-year-old daughter Hester was seeing a farmhand named Williams and banned her from his house. Distraught, his daughter threw herself into a pond in her parents' orchard, where she floated temporarily until; "her garments, heavy with their drink, pulled the poor wretch to muddy death". Found guilty of suicide, her body was buried by torchlight just before midnight, as custom dictated, whilst bystanders struggled to prevent Williams throwing himself into the grave. Commentators likened her plight to that of Hamlet's Ophelia: "hold off the earth awhile till I have caught her once more in my arms". Hester Tilly is listed in the 1841 census as working as a servant at Horfield parsonage; her father William, who was born in Yatton around 1789, remarried in July 1846 to Elizabeth Pearcy and they had a daughter Elizabeth junior the same year.

## MIXING WITH THE CLERGY

BEFORE the kick-off of Rovers' league game with Luton Town in September 1926, the Bishop of St. Albans, Rt. Rev. Michael Furse, gave a public address on the pitch as part of Luton Mission Week. Fred Hodgkinson, who played for Rovers during the inaugural 1883/84 season, was later a clergyman in Worsley, Lancashire, whilst Norman Hallam, a Port Vale player against Rovers on two occasions in the 1940s, was a Methodist minister from 1948. Kevin Street, a midfielder who played in 21 (plus twelve as substitute) league matches for Rovers, scoring twice between November 2002 and October 2003, took a four-year correspondence course at St. John's, Nottingham from 2002, then took a degree in theology at Chester University from 2006 with the intention of being ordained to the priesthood. He later worked as a teacher. Ten players with the name Bishop have opposed Rovers, the only goalscorer being Orient's Sid Bishop whose forty-yard rocket contributed to Rovers' 3-2 defeat at Brisbane Road in February 1961. Northampton Town's Charlie Bishop was sent off against Rovers at the Memorial Stadium in March 1998. Whilst Parsons and Beadle have both played for Rovers, opponents have included Vickers, Deacon, Abbott, Prior, Friar, Archdeacon, Cannon, Priest, Sexton, Monk and three Popes. Tom Pope scored for Barrow against Rovers in the FA Cup in November 2006 and for Crewe Alexandra against Rovers the following season.

## FANCY A GAME, MATE?

WHEN Rovers played Clevedon in December 1889, a match that was won 2-0, the side found itself a man short. As a result, Charles Henry Young, a Clevedon player, appeared in Rovers' line-up at outside-left that day. Born in Wrington in the summer of 1870, the son of George and Sarah Young, Charles Young lived with his parents at Dial Hill, Clevedon up until his death in 1906 at the age of just 36. Similarly, Tom Haycock, a player with Wolverton, then a powerful side, was borrowed when Rovers were a man short against Swindon Athletic in December 1893. Born in the sleepy railway town of Wolverton, Buckinghamshire in the early months of 1872, he was the seventh of eight children to Thomas, a railway signalman, and Ann Haycock, and worked as a railway carriage wood turner. Tom Haycock married a Northamptonshire girl, Minnie, and their daughter Lilian was born in 1898.

## CROWD DISTURBANCES

THERE was trouble at two reserve games, against Portsmouth and Luton Town in 1922. In January 1924, a drunken spectator attacked referee R R Crump at half-time, as Rovers trailed 3-2 to Bournemouth; he was ejected and Rovers were reported. A similar incident occurred at home to Norwich City in October 1931 when, trailing 1-0, Rovers had a late penalty appeal turned down; the referee in question was Stanley Rous, later FIFA president. Chelsea supporters pushed down a small wall at the Muller Road End at Eastville when their side lost 3-0 in February 1980. Sixty police officers were deployed to quell trouble at Exeter in January 1984 when Rovers supporters charged on to the pitch; six policemen were injured and 24 troublemakers were arrested. The FA investigated events at Ashton Gate after Peter Beadle's injury-time equaliser in an intense local derby sparked a pitch invasion seen across the world on satellite television. Two spectators attacked Stoke City's keeper Gavin Ward during the 3-3 draw at the Memorial Stadium in April 2000, after which Rovers were given a suspended two-point penalty and a £10,000 fine. A coin was thrown by a Barrow fan in Rovers' FA Cup tie at Holker Street in November 2006, missing Rovers' goalkeeper Steve Phillips.

## NO GOAL IN AGES

AFTER Mickey Evans scored after 87 minutes against Plymouth Argyle on 9th January 2001, no one would have expected the side to go 576 minutes of league action without scoring. Rovers' next goal was scored by Vitalijs Astafjevs after 33 minutes of the game against Cambridge United on February 24th 2001. This tally of 576 minutes eclipsed the previous worst run of 560 minutes between Sam Furniss' 75th-minute strike against Southend United on October 7th 1922 and Tom Howarth's fifth-minute goal against Charlton Athletic on November 5th 1922. The longest gap between league goals scored by Rovers away from home is 689 minutes from Chris Lines' 56th-minute goal at Charlton Athletic in November 2009 to Jo Kuffour's strike after 25 minutes at Swindon Town in March 2010. This beat 646 minutes from Kevin Gall's 38th-minute goal at Lincoln City in September 2001 to Martin Cameron's 54th-minute penalty at Rushden & Diamonds that December, and the 580 minutes from Steve White's goal after 35 minutes at Bolton Wanderers in February 1986, to Trevor Morgan's 75th-minute strike at Bury that April.

## OLYMPIC GAMES

IN September 1922, Rovers took Mohamed Mokhtar on trial, who had played for Egypt at football in the 1920 Olympic Games in Antwerp. Ben Iroha, a gold medallist with Nigeria at the 1996 Olympics, came to Rovers on trial in September 1998. Outside-left Arthur Hall, who played twice in the league for Rovers, played in an England Olympic trial match in April 1958; likewise, Tony Edge, having played in Olympic trials at Bisham Abbey in 1960 rejected an Olympic place in favour of a professional contract with Rovers. Bob Bearpark, a former Rovers youth player, coached the Canadian football team in the 1984 Olympic Games. Belgium's national coach at the 1912 Olympics was Billy Maxwell, who played against Rovers before World War I with both Bristol City and Millwall. George Raynor, who coached Sweden to gold in 1948 and bronze in 1952, played in both Aldershot's league games against Rovers in 1938/39. Arthur Knight, who played against Rovers for Portsmouth in the Southern League, FA Cup and, after 1920, the Football League, won a gold medal for football with England at the 1912 Olympics in Stockholm, as did Reading's centre-half in 1921/22 Ted Hanney. Bobby Brown, with Watford against Rovers in April 1963, played for England at the 1960 Olympics, whilst Dave Bamber (Swindon Town and Blackpool) represented Britain at the 1979 World Student Games.

## TURNING JAPANESE

WHILE no Japanese national has appeared for Rovers, Graham Withey, who had scored ten goals in 19 (plus three as substitute) league matches for Rovers in the 1982/83 season, played for Seiko on loan from Coventry City from October 1984. Several opponents have pursued careers in Japan. Mark Bowen, at Shimizu S-Pulse in 1997, played for Wigan Athletic against Rovers in September 1999. Jeroen Boere, who played for Southend United against Rovers in 1997/98, spent the following campaign at Omiya Ardija, where he scored nine goals in 11 matches. Kim Grant – who played for Luton Town, Charlton Athletic and Millwall against Rovers in the league, and Yeovil Town in the Football League Trophy – also played for the Japanese side Shonan Bellmere in 2005. Gordon Milne, a Liverpool player against Rovers in 1961/62, was manager at Nagoya Grampus Eight from 1994. Steve Perryman, who played three times for Brentford against Rovers in the late 1980s, later worked in Japan.

## REPRESENTING TWO NATIONS

NINE opponents have played international football for more than one country and in every case the men represented Irish and Northern Irish sides. There is a long list of dual internationalists, but those involved in the complex political arena of central Europe in the 1930s or the break-up of the Russian empire in the early 1990s never opposed Rovers in third-tier football. The only Rovers player who represented two countries in international football was Matt O'Mahony, who played in 101 league games for Rovers between 1936 and 1939, scoring six times; he won six caps for Ireland and one for Northern Ireland.

Bud Aherne .............................Eire (16 caps), Northern Ireland (6 caps)
.......................................Luton Town (4 league games v. Rovers, 1953-56)
Jackie Brown.................................Eire (2 caps, 1 goal), Northern Ireland
.................................. (10 caps, 1 goal) Coventry City and Ipswich Town
............................................... (4 league games, 1 goal v Rovers, 1948-50)
Harry Duggan........Eire (5 caps, 1 goal), Ireland (8 caps) Norwich City
..........................................................(3 league games v. Rovers, 1936-39)
Tommy Eglington..... Eire (24 caps, 2 goals), Northern Ireland (6 caps)
.................................Everton (2 league games, 1 goal v. Rovers, 1953/54)
Tom Farquharson.................Ireland (7 caps), Eire (4 caps) Cardiff City
..........................................................(7 league games v. Rovers, 1931-35)
Rory Keane.................................. Eire (4 caps), Northern Ireland (1 cap)
.................................Swansea Town (4 league games v. Rovers, 1947-54)
Mick O'Brien .......................................... Ireland (10 caps), Eire (4 caps)
...............................................QPR, Walsall, Norwich City and Watford
........................................... (11 league games, 2 goals v. Rovers, 1920-33)
Jackie O'Driscoll ........................Eire (3 caps), Northern Ireland (3 caps
.................... Swansea Town (3 league games, 1 goal v. Rovers, 1947-49)
Reg Ryan .....................Eire (16 caps, 3 goals), Northern Ireland (1 cap)
.................................Derby C (2 league games, 1 goal v. Rovers, 1957/58)

## SINGERS

COVENTRY City, when known as Singers FC, lost an extraordinary game 7-6 at Eastville in December 1899. Jack Lewis scored a second-half hat-trick as Rovers, having been level at 4-4 at half-time, seized a remarkable victory.

# GOODNIGHT IRENE

FOR many beyond the confines of the Memorial Stadium, an awareness of the role of Goodnight Irene in all things Bristol Rovers and an understanding of its significance is something of a mystery. Yet, unlike the story of many club songs, the tale of this crowd favourite appears to have a clear beginning. On November 4th 1950, Plymouth Argyle arrived at Eastville with an accordion player, who performed contemporary songs around the edge of the pitch prior to the start of the match. One of these songs was the Huddie William 'Lead Belly' Ledbetter record Goodnight Irene, sung by Argyle supporters by dint of the fact that The Weavers, featuring Pete Seeger, had released their own version on May 26th 1950, which reached number one in the American charts. As Argyle took a first-half lead, their supporters used the song to taunt home fans. Three Rovers goals in eight second-half minutes provoked a rendition of Goodnight Argyle and the song soon caught on. When Rovers played at Newcastle United before a crowd of 62,787 in the club's first-ever FA Cup quarter-final in the spring of 1951, the Magpies bowed to pressure and played the Jo Stafford rendition of the song during the pre-match build-up. Down the years, many singers have produced cover versions of this song, including Frank Sinatra, Rolf Harris and the England centre-half Billy Wright.

# THE LEGEND OF JOE WALTER

THE only Rovers player to live to the age of 99 was Joe Walter. Born in Bristol in August 1895, he joined the club from local football and scored 12 times from inside-forward in 82 league matches between 1920 and 1922, and during the 1928-29 season. Also with Blackburn Rovers and Huddersfield Town, it was with the latter that he secured two league championship medals, playing under the great Herbert Chapman. A supporter of Rovers events for many years, Joe Walter died in 1995, just months short of his hundredth birthday. The only opponent to face Rovers in league football who has lived to be 100 was Zillwood George March, known as 'Zach' (1892-1994), who played twice for Brighton & Hove Albion against Rovers over Christmas 1921.

# THOUSAND

ROVERS' thousandth league game was the goalless draw at Plymouth Argyle in March 1951; the thousandth at home was the 1-1 draw with Port Vale in October 1973, and the thousandth away the goalless draw at Hereford United later that month. Rovers' thousandth league goal was scored by inside-forward Les Golledge, the only goal of his career, in a 6-1 victory over Exeter City at Eastville in April 1936. The thousandth conceded was Luton Town's third in their 6-2 win at Kenilworth Road in January 1935. Southend United's thousandth league game was the 1-1 draw with Rovers in March 1951, while their thousandth home league game was the goalless draw with Rovers in November 1972. Bournemouth's thousandth league game was their 2-0 win against Rovers in March 1951 and Ipswich Town's thousandth was their match against Rovers in January 1992. Rovers' 2,000th league game was the goalless draw at home to York City in October 1973 and the 3,000th was the 3-1 victory away to Hull City in February 1996. Preston North End became, after Notts County, the second team to play in 4,000 fixtures, reaching this landmark in their 2-2 draw with Rovers at the Memorial Stadium in September 1998. When the return fixture was drawn 2-2 at Deepdale five months later Preston became the first side to have drawn a thousand league matches.

# COLD TURKEY

THERE are few tales quite like the Paddy Molloy story. Born in Rossendale in 1909, he ran away to join the army before working as a fairground boxer. Turning to football, he played for Fulham before appearing in six games for Rovers as a centre-half in the 1933/34 season and went on to play for Cardiff City, Queens Park Rangers, Stockport County, Carlisle United and Bradford City before trying his luck in Northern Irish football. After the war, following one final appearance for Notts County, Molloy became manager of the Turkish national side in 1949. On one occasion, he was asked to referee a championship decider in Turkey and, having sent a player off, abandoned the game when a penalty decision prompted a pitch invasion. Turning down an offer to coach Chile, Molloy joined Watford, where he worked in various guises for many years, seeing the side rise from Division Four to the First Division. He died in St. Albans in February 1993.

## PLAYING AGAINST ROVERS

A LOYAL, one-club man, 'Tug' Wilson played in 509 league matches for Brighton & Hove Albion between 1922 and 1936, scoring 67 goals. An outside-left born in Yorkshire in July 1899, he died in 1955, having played in 23 league matches against Rovers – more than any other opponent in the Football League era – scoring four times. In many of these matches for Brighton he was accompanied by Bobby Farrell, the only other player to have played in as many as 20 league games against Rovers for one club. Ian Wood scored three league goals against Rovers and they all came in the same match.

Ernie 'Tug' Wilson .. 23 .................................... Brighton & Hove Albion
Roger Jones .............. 21 ..Bournemouth, Blackburn R., Stoke C., Derby ............................................................................... Co., York C.
Roy Tunks ................. 21 ...Preston NE, Rotherham United, Wigan Ath.
Reg Wilkinson ........ 21 ...................................... Brighton, Norwich City
Bobby Farrell ........... 20 .................................... Brighton & Hove Albion
Harry Morris ........... 20 .................. Brentford, Millwall, Swindon Town
Ian Wood ................. 20 .................... Mansfield Town, Oldham Athletic

## PINK SHIRTS

AN April Fool's Day hoax on the club website in 2005 indicated that Rovers were to take stock of a set of pink shirts. This idea was swiftly taken on board by a number of the club's supporters through the fans' forum on the internet and support for this unusual and unlikely idea gradually grew. Pressure was put on the club to make this extraordinary concept real and Rovers agreed to issue a limited edition pink club shirt. These shirts were snapped up swiftly and can now be found at extortionate prices on internet sites. Several wags suggested that, to mark Rovers' appearance at Shrewsbury Town's Gay Meadow, it would be appropriate for Rovers to wear pink. The opportunity, though, was not taken and Oldham Athletic, who wore neon pink for their game against Leeds United in March 2009 to raise money for charity, became the first side in recent years to appear in pink shirts in a Football League fixture.

## WORLD CUP SEMI-FINALS

AS with finals, only one man has played for Rovers in the league and appeared in a World Cup semi-final for his country – Alan Ball. A total of 12 players have opposed Rovers in league action and also appeared in a World Cup semi-final: six of England's 1966 team, Alan Ball, Jack Charlton, George Cohen, Bobby Moore, Ray Wilson and Roger Hunt; four of England's 1990 side, Trevor Steven, Peter Beardsley, Peter Shilton and Chris Waddle; Roland Nilsson, who played for Sweden in 1994 and for Sheffield Wednesday against Rovers in October 1990; and Bontcho Guentchev, who appeared for Bulgaria in 1994 and was sent off at the Memorial Stadium in February 1997, when playing for Luton Town. Six other players appeared against Rovers in cup football – Terry Butcher, Paul Gascoigne, Gordon Banks, Geoff Hurst, Bobby Charlton and Martin Peters. Gary Lineker scored for England in the 1990 semi-final, and for Leicester City reserves, against Rovers reserves in November 1983. A special mention must also be made of Sandy Wood, who played for the United States when they lost 6-1 to Argentina in the semi-final of the inaugural World Cup in 1930 and played at Eastville in March 1938 when Colchester United lost 2-1 to Rovers reserves in a Southern League match.

## SCHOOLTEACHERS

A NUMBER of Rovers players have gone into teaching, including club founder Bill Somerton. Bill Braund, another founder member of the Black Arabs, taught at Mina Road School, Anglesea Place School and Russell Town School, and was headmaster of Barleyfields Board School, from 1905 to 1927. In addition, five inter-war players became teachers: Bert Blake (Eastville Boys' School), Vivian Gibbins (head of Harold Road School, West Ham), Charles Littlewood (Badminton School), Les Berry (cricket coach at Uppingham School), and David Murray (football and hockey coach at Victoria College on the Channel Islands). Since World War II, Harry Haddon taught in Bradford-upon-Avon, Roy James taught at Henbury Court School and was later headmaster of Ashton Court School and Charborough Road School in Filton, Kevin Street taught in Cheshire and David Williams taught at Mostyn High School in Cardiff. Harry Bamford's tragically early death in a motor accident came as he travelled home from coaching schoolboys at Clifton College in October 1958.

## PHANTOM WHISTLER

JUST after half-time in the game at home to Brentford in October 1996, the visiting goalkeeper Kevin Dearden heard a whistle from the crowd. Wrongly believing that the referee had stopped play, he halted, allowing Rovers' eagle-eyed midfielder Marcus Browning to nip in and score. Rovers won this league match 2-1, before a crowd of 5,163, with striker Jamie Cureton having scored Rovers' opening goal.

## DISALLOWED GOALS

FOUR goals were disallowed during Rovers' 2-0 defeat at Grimsby Town in a Third Division match played in January 1973. Alan Gauden (2), and Stuart Brace for the home side, as well as Rovers' Bruce Bannister, all saw 'goals' ruled out for foul play or offside. Phil Hubbard and David Booth both scored goals in a match watched by a crowd of 8,975.

## SCORING AND CONCEDING

WHILST playing for Rotherham United at home to Bournemouth in October 1972, former Rovers striker Carl Gilbert scored twice and then, as an emergency goalkeeper, conceded three in a 7-2 defeat. Gilbert had scored 15 goals in 45 league games for Rovers after signing from Gillingham in 1969.

## BIRTHDAY HAT-TRICK

NOT noted for his prolific scoring, defender Neil Arndale did not find the net in his five league appearances for Rovers. However, on his 20th birthday in April 2004, he scored a first-half volley and two second-half penalties to complete a hat-trick as Rovers reserves lost 5-3 to Oxford United reserves.

## PUNCHING THE REFEREE

REFEREE A. J. Attwood booked Plymouth Argyle reserves centre-half Jack Pullen, a former Welsh international, and then sent him off, during the Western League game against Rovers reserves in October 1928. Pullen punched the referee twice, in the process giving him a cut lip and swollen eye, although Mr Attwood continued resolutely with the game.

## YOURA ESHAYA

AT some point in 1933, and probably in Iran, Youra Eshaya was born to Iranian parents, one of six children of Eshaya Pera and Batishwa Benyamin. They fled Iran in 1935 and settled in Iraq at Hinaidi where, as early as 1952, young Youra was being dubbed 'Iraq's greatest footballer' (Andrious Mam Jotyar, *The Iran Times*). He played for Levy Civilian and also for RAF Habbaniya and was spotted by a Rovers scout scoring a hat-trick for an Iraqi Command XI against an RAF Suez XI in April 1953. Manager Bert Tann brought him to Bristol in August 1954 and he remained with Rovers for 18 months, scoring four goals in 28 games for the Colts and once in three outings for Rovers reserves. Eshaya returned to Iraq in December 1955 to play for the Iraqi Air Force XI and won his first cap for Iraq in January 1956, scoring in a 6-0 win against a Teheran XI, the first of 75 international caps. He married Elizabeth in 1971, a Swedish national and, ostracised as she was a non-Muslim, was obliged to emigrate to Sweden in 1972, where they had three children. This Iranian-born Rovers trialist died on a football pitch in July 1992, at the age of 59, after suffering a heart attack whilst coaching Gothenburg schoolchildren.

## FIFTY-TWO PINTS OF BEER

PERHAPS the most bizarre transfer deal involving a Rovers player was that of Ted Hough. He had joined Southampton in October 1921 for the unlikely fee of 52 pints of beer, that being the size of the round the Saints' management bought for Talbot Stead Works of Walsall before they would consider any offer for the full-back. Joining Rovers later in his career, he was to play in one league game, against Reading in 1933. The former Rovers full-back Donnie Gillies had the unusual experience of twice signing for Trowbridge Town and yet never playing for them in any fixture. Tim Parkin joined Rovers in 1981 at a time when Swedish-based players were not allowed to move to professional clubs outside Sweden. For this reason, Parkin was technically an Almondsbury Greenway player for half an hour before joining Rovers in a £15,000 deal. Goalkeeper Dick Sheppard left Rovers to Torquay United on loan in December 1973 at an evening roadside rendezvous near Bridgwater.

## NEVER MISSED A GAME

TWO players have been ever-present in a league season for Rovers on five separate occasions. Goalkeeper Jesse Whatley did not miss a game in five years during the mid-1920s and Ray Warren, who had played for the club before World War II, appeared in every match in five of the immediate post-war seasons, culminating in the 1952/53 season, when he captained the side to the Third Division (South) championship. The following players have played in every match in three or more seasons with Rovers during their careers:

| | | |
|---|---|---|
| 5 ...Ray Warren | ............. | 1946/47, 1948/49, 1949/50, 1950/51, 1952/53 |
| ......Jesse Whatley | .......... | 1922/23, 1923/24, 1924/25, 1925/26, 1926/27 |
| 4 ...Jackie Pitt | ................................ | 1947/48, 1951/52, 1952/53, 1954/55 |
| ......Stuart Taylor | ............................ | 1969/70, 1970/71, 1971/72, 1973/74 |
| 3 ...Harry Bamford | ....................................... | 1952/53, 1955/56, 1957/58 |
| ......Geoff Fox | ................................................ | 1949/50, 1951/52, 1952/53 |
| ......Peter Sampson | ........................................ | 1950/51, 1951/52, 1952/53 |
| ......Geoff Twentyman | .................................... | 1988/89, 1989/90, 1990/91 |

## GREYHOUND RACING

NOT only did Rovers play on the nearest league pitch to a motorway, but the ground at Eastville was also one of the leading greyhound tracks in the country. In March 1932, the Bristol Greyhound Racing Association became a public company and rented Eastville from Rovers, with the option of first refusal if the ground were ever to be sold. The first race took place there in July 1932. During World War II, it is perfectly feasible that Rovers would have folded, had the greyhound company not continued to provide the club with income and, in March 1940, Rovers chairman Fred Ashmead took the unilateral decision to sell the ground to the tenants for £12,000. When, in 1986, the greyhound company refused Rovers' tenancy, a fourth weekly meeting was added so that it temporarily became the busiest track in the United Kingdom. The final race meeting took place at Eastville in October 1997, with entry fees waived, and the furniture giants IKEA moved on site in March 1999.

## HIGHEST DRAWS

ROVERS have been involved in two ten-goal draws in league football and have, on eight occasions, played in a drawn league match that included eight goals. The most extraordinary of these was the game against Leeds United in 1960, when Rovers trailed 4-0 at the interval.

Rovers 5 Exeter City 5 .......................... D3(S) .................. 10/11/34
Rovers 5 Charlton Ath. 5 ..................... D2 ...................... 18/11/78
Fulham 4 Rovers 4 ............................... D2 ...................... 20/08/53
Rovers 4 Swansea Town 4 .................... D2 ...................... 30/03/59
Rovers 4 Leeds United 4 ...................... D2 ...................... 29/08/60
Rovers 4 Port Vale 4 ............................. D3 ...................... 28/12/63
Rovers 4 Mansfield Town 4 ................. D3 ...................... 15/10/66
Rovers 4 Exeter City 4 ......................... D3 ...................... 29/12/82
Oldham Ath. 4 Rovers 4 ...................... D2 ...................... 27/09/97
Rovers 4 Mansfield Town 4 ................. L2 ...................... 19/03/05

## DELAYED BY THE CRICKET

STAN Prout's Rovers debut kicked off at half past six in the evening. The reason for this was that Sussex were playing at home to Australia at Hove on the same day, the opening day of the 1934/35 football season. Once the cricket was completed, Rovers started their new season at neighbouring Brighton and proceeded to lose 3-1 before a crowd of 12,000, Jimmy Smith scoring Rovers' consolation goal. Prout, a summer signing from Chelsea, was to play in 39 league matches for Rovers, scoring five goals, before moving to Chester City in 1936.

## LOTTERY

ANDY Spring, who played at full-back for Rovers during the 1985/86 season, bought a 25p ticket on the Irish National Lottery in 1992 and won £250,000. Bobby Sibbald, who played at full-back for Southport in both their fixtures against Rovers in 1973/74, won a major windfall on the United States lottery in the early 1990s.

## TRUMPTON

ROVERS played home games at Twerton Park, Bath between 1986 and 1996. Home to Bath City since 1932, Twerton Park had a ground attendance record of 18,020 from Bath City's FA Cup tie against Brighton & Hove Albion in January 1960. The first league game played there was Rovers' 1-0 win against Bolton Wanderers in August 1986, Trevor Morgan scoring from a penalty. The final game was a 1-0 win against Peterborough United in August 1996, Andy Gurney scoring the goal. Rovers played in 231 league matches at Twerton Park, winning 111 and losing 47, scoring 359 goals and conceding 248. The highest league win was 6-1 against Wigan Athletic in March 1990 and the heaviest defeat 5-1 at the hands of Barnsley in November 1992. Carl Saunders was the only player to score four times in a game on the ground, his strikes easing Rovers to a 5-0 FA Cup win against Bath City in November 1994. Only two opponents – Brentford's Joe Allon in 1994 and Swindon Town's Kevin Horlock the following year – scored hat-tricks there. Bristol City were the only side to play in as many as eight league fixtures on the ground, while only Bournemouth and Swindon Town achieved three away wins; Wolverhampton Wanderers drew all four of their league matches at the ground.

## WORLD CUP FINAL

ONLY one man has won a World Cup winner's medal, and also played league football for Rovers. Alan Ball was the all-action midfield dynamo in England's 1966 triumph and also played in 17 league matches for Rovers in the 1982/83 season, scoring twice. The first league game played in by any of England's 1966 side was when Jack Charlton played for Leeds United against Doncaster Rovers in April 1953; the final game was when Alan Ball played for Rovers against Cardiff City in May 1983. Seven players who have played in a World Cup Final have opposed Rovers in league football; Alan Ball, Jack Charlton, George Cohen, Bobby Moore, Ray Wilson and Roger Hunt (England, 1966) and Nestor Lorenzo, a member of Argentina's 1990 side who played for Swindon Town in the 1990/91 season. In addition, Gordon Banks, Geoff Hurst, Bobby Charlton and Martin Peters all opposed Rovers in League Cup ties, while Jack Charlton, Geoff Hurst and Ossie Ardiles, a winner in 1978 with Argentina, all managed sides in league fixtures against Rovers.

## IAN HOLLOWAY

SOMETHING of the epitome of a local hero, 'Olly' Holloway enjoyed three playing spells with Rovers and was later the club's manager. A hugely influential midfield maestro during the 1989/90 Third Division championship season, Holloway scored a number of crucial goals at Eastville, and at Twerton Park. In May 1990, he calmly converted a much-delayed penalty against Bristol City in Bath to help secure the club's long-awaited promotion back to the second tier of domestic English football. His 14th birthday coincided with new national regulations and, as a result, he became the first player in the country to sign associate schoolboy forms when he signed for Rovers in 1977. His debut came at Wrexham in April 1981 and the 18-year-old Holloway featured in the youngest Rovers side ever to take the field. With the club from 1981-85, 1987-91 and 1996-99, he totalled 379 (plus 18 as substitute) league matches for Rovers and scored 42 league goals. Returning to the club as manager in May 1996, he was in charge for almost five years, before taking over at Queens Park Rangers, one of his former clubs, Plymouth Argyle, Leicester City and Blackpool. Ian Holloway remains a great credit to his profession on and off the field and is one of the most popular figures from Rovers' long and varied history.

## EURO GLORY

FIVE Rovers players have played in European club competition finals with other clubs:

| | | | | |
|---|---|---|---|---|
| 1966/67.... | UEFA Cup | .........Terry Cooper | ...... Leeds U | ....runners-up |
| 1967/68.... | UEFA Cup | .........Terry Cooper | ...... Leeds U | ......... winners |
| 1970/71.... | UEFA Cup | .........Terry Cooper | ...... Leeds U | ......... winners |
| 1971/72.... | UEFA Cup | .........Kenny Hibbitt | .... Wolves | ......runners-up |
| 1972/73.... | UEFA Cup | .........Larry Lloyd | ......... Liverpool | .......winners |
| 1978/79.... | European Cup | ....Larry Lloyd | ......... N'ham F. | .......winners |
| 1979/80.... | European Cup | ....Larry Lloyd | ......... N'ham F. | .......winners |
| 1983/84.... | UEFA Cup | .........Gary Mabbutt | .... Spurs | .............winners |
| 2009/10.... | Europa Lge | .........Bobby Zamora | .... Fulham | .....runners-up |

IAN HOLLOWAY WAS A POPULAR PLAYER AND MANAGER WITH ROVERS

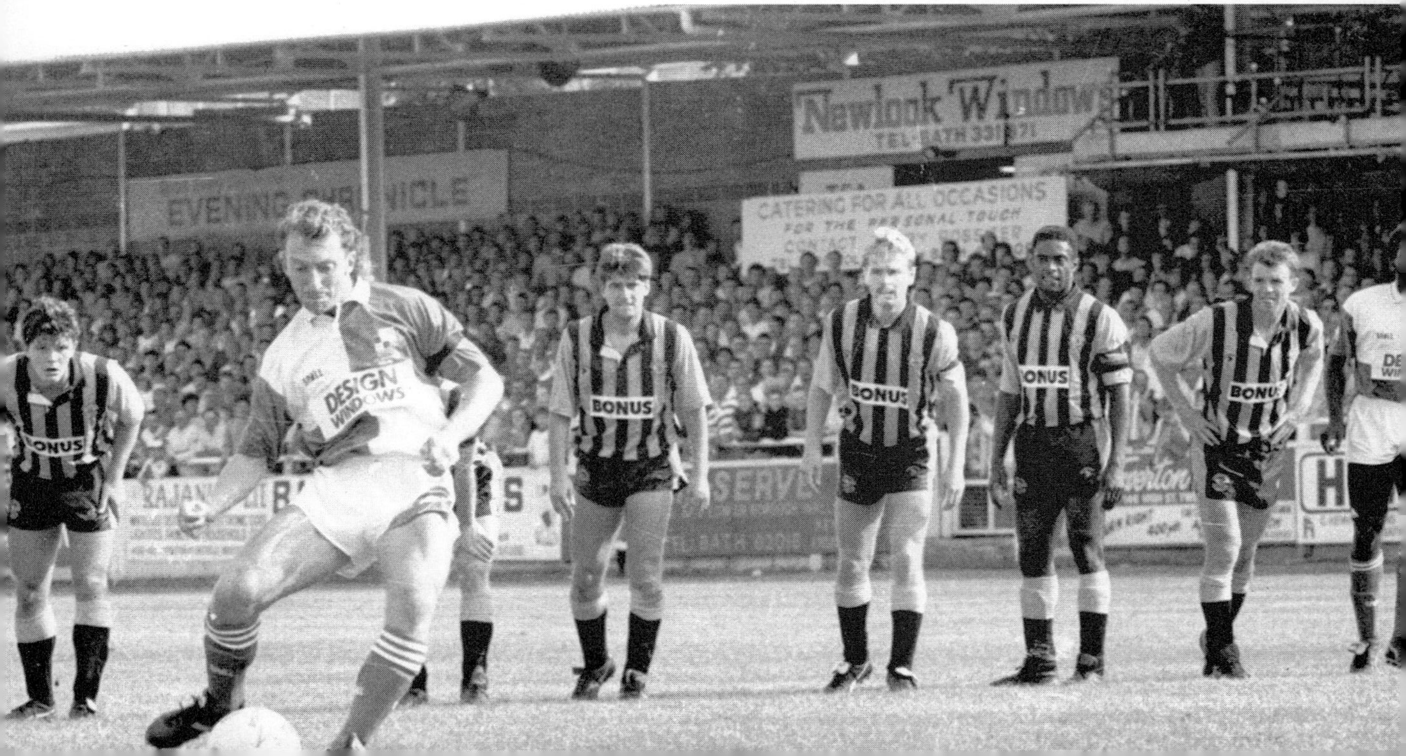

## SUB PEN

IT is a relative rarity that a substitute scores from the penalty spot. Two Rovers players and four opponents have achieved this feat in competitive football. Mark Walters' goal against Oxford United in 2001 was one of two goals he scored that day; Dwayne Plummer also missed a penalty for Rovers earlier in the game. Paul Heffernan's was the second penalty Rovers conceded at Doncaster as Brian Stock had scored their opening goal. Anthony Pulis, in his sole appearance in a Rovers shirt, was booked for the foul that led to the second penalty.

Dean Saunders ... Swansea City 2 Rovers 0 ........22/01/1985 .. FLC
Peter Beadle ....... Southend United 1 Rovers 1 .. 22/11/1997 ..... FL
Mark Robertson  Swindon Town 1 Rovers 3 ..... 21/10/2000 ..... FL
Mark Walters ..... Rovers 6 Oxford United 2 ...... 21/04/2001 ..... FL
Simon Johnson  .. Darlington 1 Rovers 1 ............ 11/02/2006 ..... FL
Paul Heffernan  .. Doncaster Rovers 2 Rovers 0 .09/02/2008 ..... FL

## NOT QUITE A GAME

ONLY four one-game wonders did not complete their sole league appearance in a Rovers shirt. In the cases of Ryan Morgan and Tony Obi, they started the game but were later substituted for tactical reasons and never reappeared in the side. Wayne Andrews played only the first 17 minutes of Rovers' game at Huish Park before succumbing to an injury in a tackle by Terry Skiverton that halted his Rovers career; he later returned to the Football League with Yeovil Town, when signed by Skiverton himself. Irishman Brian Cash was a late substitute against Northampton Town but was substituted before the end of the match.

Wayne Andrews ......................................... 29/03/08 v Yeovil Town
Brian Cash ..................................... 03/01/05 v Northampton Town
Ryan Morgan ................................................... 18/03/97 v Watford
Tony Obi ............................................. 07/09/85 v Newport County

## SUBSTITUTES SEEING RED

| | | |
|---|---|---|
| Uwe Hartenberger | 26/01/1994 | Rovers 1 Reading 1 D2 |
| Steven Reid | 26/12/1999 | Rovers 1 Millwall 0 D2 |
| Ben Petty | 16/12/2000 | Rovers 0 Stoke City 3 D2 |
| Richard Gell | 27/11/2001 | Rovers 1 Aldershot 0 FAC |
| Trevor Challis | 08/12/2001 | Plymouth A. 1 Rovers 1 FAC |
| Simon Bryant | 20/09/2003 | York City 2 Rovers 1 D3 |
| Jake Edwards | 13/12/2003 | Rovers 0 Yeovil Town 1 D3 |
| Sofiane Zaaboub | 24/11/2007 | Swindon Town 1 Rovers 0 L1 |
| Richard Walker | 24/11/2007 | Swindon Town 1 Rovers 0 L1 |
| Fabien Brandy | 18/03/2008 | Rovers 0 Swansea City 2 L1 |
| Jabo Ibehre | 27/11/2008 | Rovers 3 Orient 3 FAC |
| Glenn Murray | 24/04/2010 | Brighton 2 Rovers 1 L1 |

## THE TALE OF BILL VOSPER

WHEN Bill Vosper turned out as outside-right for Rovers against St. George in March 1890 it was to be his sole appearance for the club. William Samuel Vosper had been born in Tewkesbury in 1867, the oldest of five children to William Samuel Vosper senior and Mary Ann Walker, who had married in Upton-upon-Severn the previous year. His father moved the family to Bristol as he worked in the pub trade and took over the Lord Nelson in Lower Ashley Road, St. Paul's, in 1891. Bill junior married Anna Maria Vaughan in the summer of 1895 and the couple had three daughters, Gladys, Millicent and Alice, all born around the turn of the century. Sadly, Bill senior died in 1901 at the age of 57 and the former Rovers player took on the running of the pub. However, ill health forced him to hand over the reins in 1906 and he was to die in Bristol over the summer of 1908, aged just 40. The Lord Nelson shut down in the 1960s.

## COUNTDOWN

NOT content with four (plus one as substitute) Football League appearances and one goal for Rovers, and six full caps for Northern Ireland, striker Adrian Coote became the first former Rovers player to appear on the television show *Countdown*. Former Blackpool defender Clarke Carlisle and one-time Cambridge United midfielder Neil MacKenzie were both *Countdown* winners in their time.

## SEVERE WEATHER

IF you ever wonder why you are standing in torrential rain or freezing conditions, it is worth recalling a few Rovers games from the past. In January 1925, Rovers lost 2-0 at home to Northampton Town in a game almost entirely lost in dense fog, to the extent that the identity of the first goalscorer is heavily disputed. The reporters on the touchline could not even see the goalmouth, let alone tell whether Bill Poyntz or, as seems more likely, Ernie Cockle, had given the visitors the lead. When the sides met again in December 1928, Rovers lost to an own goal from the unfortunate Jack Cosgrove, whose innocuous backpass was completely missed in dense fog by Rovers' goalkeeper Jesse Whatley and trickled into the net for a bizarre winning goal. The game at Southend United in January 1932 was also played in fog, whilst Rovers and Gillingham forfeited their half-time in March 1927 to complete a league fixture in severe wind and rain. Rovers' 5-2 defeat at West Ham United in September 1954 was played out in torrential rain and a thunderstorm. The weather was so inclement in the 1962/63 season that Rovers ended up playing in nine league fixtures in April and a further five in May.

## LEYLAND DAF TROPHY

ROVERS have twice reached the final of this tournament for third- and fourth-tier English league sides. In a variety of guises and under a range of sponsors, the competition has offered the chance of a big day out to sides that would not otherwise enjoy such high-profile occasions. Rovers first appeared in this tournament in the 1983/84 season, when it was known as the Associate Members' Cup, and beat Newport County 1-0 in their first game. In May 1990, Rovers went down 2-1 to Tranmere Rovers in the Wembley final in front of 48,402 spectators, and in 2007 lost 3-2 to Doncaster Rovers before a crowd of 59,025 at the Millennium Stadium. Ian Holloway has played in a club record 22 matches in this competition, while Marcus Stewart has top-scored with nine goals. Rovers' largest win was 4-2 against Cambridge United in November 1994 and the heaviest defeat was 3-0 to Bristol City in December 1986. Paul Vassell, Carl Metcalfe, Lee Portch and Matt Hope appeared for Rovers in this tournament, but never in league football.

# NAMES

SOME spectacularly named players have represented Rovers down the years. Kossuth Barnes, a goalkeeper in the 1921/22 season, was named after a Hungarian revolutionary, Lajos Kossuth, who died in 1894. Ashley Griffiths, a 1980s full-back, was named after the Australian tennis player Ashley Cooper. Rovers' inter-war centre-forward Albert Kitchener Iles, 1920s full-back Ernest Baden Sambidge and Devon Winston White owed their middle names to celebrated war heroes or politicians. A fast and elusive winger from 1993, Worrell Sterling is named after the former West Indies cricket captain, Sir Frank Worrell. The early-1980s centre-forward Errington Edison Kelly's middle name reflected that of a contemporary African politician, Edison Mundarawaywa. Others picked up sporting nicknames because of perceived physical similarities – Thomas 'Tancy' Lea and Devon 'Bruno' White after contemporary boxers, and David 'Boris' Mehew after a tennis player, being prime examples. Novello Dunckley Shenton played for Rovers between 1895 and 1899, whilst Exodus Geohaghan had a trial with Rovers in October 2004. Dennis Lincoln Bailey joined Lincoln City in 1997, whilst Mark Everton Walters was formerly with Liverpool.

# PENALTY!

HUGH McBain scored the first penalty awarded to Rovers, in the game against Mangotsfield in January 1895, a 5-3 defeat in the Gloucestershire Cup. Ray Warren and Bruce Bannister each scored a club-record 17 league penalties during their time with Rovers. Stewart Barrowclough scored from the penalty spot in three consecutive league matches for Rovers in the autumn of 1979, a feat equalled by Ian Holloway in October 1990. Warren holds the club seasonal record having scored seven penalties in the 1948/49 season, a club record in the league equalled in 2009/10 by Jeff Hughes; during the 1979/80 season Rovers again scored seven penalties, Barrowclough claiming six of them, and Vaughan Jones one. Rovers conceded a club record nine penalties in the 1978/79 season. During the first four matches of 1992/93, Rovers conceded a goal from a penalty in each game. Matt Lockwood, who scored just one league goal for Rovers in 58 (plus five as substitute) league matches between 1996 and 1998, is Orient's record penalty goalscorer of all time; he was at Brisbane Road between 1998 and 2007. Rovers' reserve side missed 17 penalties during the 1952/53 season.

## GEOFF BRADFORD

THE annals of Rovers history are filled with names of great players, yet none are revered as much as Geoff Bradford. Born in Clifton in July 1927, young Geoff excelled with Soundwell and, after three years in the army, was signed as a centre-forward at Eastville. His signing proved an inspirational one. From his debut against Crystal Palace in September 1949, he began to score freely in the Third Division. His eight league hat-tricks, in addition to the four goals in a game against Rotherham United in May 1959, helped establish Rovers as a force to be reckoned with in post-war English football. A hat-trick against Newport County in April 1953 secured promotion to Division Two and left him with a club record seasonal tally of 33 league goals. In Division Two, his goalscoring continued, despite two lay-offs with a broken leg. In October 1955, he became the only man to play for England whilst on Rovers' books and he duly scored the final goal, as his country defeated Denmark 5-1 in Copenhagen. Having scored 242 league goals in 461 appearances for his only professional club, Bradford retired in May 1964 to work for an oil company. He died in Bristol in December 1994, aged 67.

## GREAT COMEBACKS

THERE have been a number of occasions in league matches featuring Rovers when one side has been three goals ahead and has not won the game. On one occasion, at Crystal Palace in March 1927, Rovers led 3-0 in a Third Division (South) fixture after just 17 minutes, but eventually lost 7-4. In August 1960, Rovers trailed 4-0 at half-time at home to Leeds United but a concerted second-half effort saw the Second Division match finish 4-4. On four occasions, Rovers have recovered a three-goal deficit to draw; twice against Ipswich Town in February 1939 and August 1991, and also against Northampton Town in September 1935, and Oldham Athletic in September 1997 – the game ending 4-4. In November 1934, Rovers led Exeter City 3-0 after 30 minutes and 5-2 after 82 minutes only to draw an eventful game 5-5. In October 1952, Rovers trailed 2-0 at Northampton Town when 90 minutes were up, only to score twice in injury time to claim an unlikely draw – Rovers next lost in the league more than five months later.

## VICTORY AT WEMBLEY

JUST before five o'clock on the last Saturday in May 2007, Sammy Igoe collected the ball on the edge of his own penalty area at the newly-reopened Wembley and made the most significant run of his footballing career. "Sixty yards, two look-ups and a slight swerve to the right later, he let go a shot that, by the time it rolled in, had secured the fourth promotion of Rovers' 87 years in the Football League." (Jamie Jackson, *The Observer*). There was a brief moment, as the ball trickled gently towards the goal line, during which the largest ever assembly of Gasheads – some 40,000 or more contributing to a Wembley crowd of 61,589, the second highest total ever at a game featuring Bristol Rovers – held its collective breath. Would it, or wouldn't it? And then came the most explosive eruption of sound. Igoe disappeared beneath a mound of players, the crowd went berserk, Goodnight Irene was sung by the collected masses and Rovers had returned to League One, so ending a dismal six seasons entrenched in the basement division. The 3-1 play-off final victory over Shrewsbury Town was the first time – in three visits to the famous ground – that Rovers had won a match at the national stadium.

## SCORED IN THE FA CUP FINAL

WHILE Rovers have on three occasions made the quarter-finals of the FA Cup, five players who have turned out for the club have scored in the final itself. The first such player was Alf Jasper Geddes, who scored for West Bromwich Albion in the 1892 final, when the Baggies defeated Aston Villa 3-0; he played for Rovers in the 1901/02 season. Jimmy Howie, a Rovers player in 1902/03, scored for Newcastle United in 1908, when they lost 3-1 to Wolves. Jack Allen also played for Newcastle, scoring both their goals in a 2-1 victory over Arsenal in 1932 before appearing for Rovers in 1934/35. Gary Mabbutt, who had been with Rovers between 1978 and 1982, scored for Spurs in the 1987 final, which was lost 3-2 to Coventry City; some records also credit an own goal to his name in the same match. Most recently, Lee Martin, who scored the only goal of the game when Manchester United defeated Crystal Palace in the FA Cup Final replay of 1990, was with Rovers during the 1996/97 season.

# MUSICIANS

A RELIABLE defender of recent years, Steve Elliott was also the drummer for The Serg, who often played in front of crowds reaching 5,000. Willie White, a Scottish inside-forward who played in eight league games for Rovers in 1928/29, was also a top-class banjo player who toured Fife with several other members of his family. Gwyn Jones, who made 153 league appearances for Rovers in the 1960s, was an excellent pianist and was awarded an advanced Musical Honour from the Royal College of Music. Ralph Jones, who played in thirteen league matches for Rovers in the late 1940s, scoring once, was a talented baritone who sang with the Glyndebourne Opera Company as well as appearing at the Edinburgh festival. Terry Cooper, later a Rovers player and manager, was a member of the 1970 England World Cup squad and their single Back Home reached number one in the charts. Dave Stone, a Rovers centre-half in the 1960s, was formerly head chorister at St. Mary Redcliffe. Rovers' striking partnership of Elvis Hammond and Nathan 'Duke' Ellington proved influential musically, but sadly lacking in goals. James Cooke, a Rovers player for the 1889/90 season, was the fourth son of James Cooke senior, a professional musician from Bath. Tarki Micallef, who played for Rovers in 1986/87, later worked as a scene shifter at the Welsh National Opera. Rod Hull, who was most famous for his partnership with Emu, and died in the spring of 1999, recorded Bristol Rovers – All the Way during the 1973/74 season to the tune of She'll Be Coming Round The Mountain. Several of Rovers' opponents possessed strong musical roots. Colin Grainger (Sunderland and Leeds United), Jack Cock (Plymouth Argyle and Millwall) and Harold 'Jazzo' Kirk (Exeter City and Plymouth Argyle) were noted singers, Kirk being also a noted ukulele player and pianist. Bert Badger – who played Southern League football against Rovers for Brentford and Watford before World War I – was an accomplished violinist. Roy Dwight, an uncle of Sir Elton John, played against Rovers for both Fulham and Coventry City, scoring Fulham's second goal in a 2-2 draw at Eastville in April 1958. Scott and Stefan Oakes, who played for Luton Town (1992/93) and Wycombe Wanderers and Notts County (2004-07) respectively, were the sons of Trevor Oakes, a founder member of Showaddywaddy. Jonathan Chiedozie Obika, who scored Yeovil Town's winning goal against Rovers in October 2009, is a first cousin of the singer Lemar.

# CLUBS

PHIL Kite, who began his career in goal for Rovers, played for thirteen different clubs in Football League action. Les Roberts was on the books of 16 league clubs, but only represented 12; he was on Rovers' books in 1921 but never played. David Byrne played for 23 league, or senior non-league, clubs and Francis Joseph, 20. Jack Pattison had 21 spells with different clubs, though this included two or three spells at the same clubs. Ten sides to which Willie White, a Rovers player in the 1928/29 season, had been attached at some stage were plying their trade in Division Three during the 1936/37 season. When Ian Hendon played for Barnet against Rovers in August 2005, he became the first opponent to have played against the club for seven different sides in league football. Justin Walker played for five different clubs against Rovers in the space of six seasons around the millennium. The most clubs an individual player has represented in one season is three; in the 2003/04 season, Andy White appeared against Rovers in the colours of Boston United and Mansfield Town as well as being an unused substitute for Kidderminster Harriers when Rovers visited Aggborough three days after Christmas Day.

# QUARTER-FINALISTS

IN the spring of 2008, Rovers, "unquestionably the Cinderella team of the FA Cup" (Dave Rogers) reached the quarter-finals of the FA Cup for only the third time in the club's history. Before a fiercely vocal record attendance of 12,011, Rovers were undone by a slick and effective West Bromwich Albion side that played with great skill, and clinical finishing in front of goal. The margin of defeat – 5-1 – was harsh on a Rovers side that competed well, but reflected the power of an Albion side who were top scorers in the four divisions of English football. Ishmael Miller, a cut above everyone else on the day, scored a well-taken hat-trick, only the second opponent ever to do so at The Memorial Stadium. For some time – after Danny Coles' scrambled goal on 31 minutes from Stuart Campbell's right-wing corner had cut the score to 2-1 – Rovers were in the tie. But "Miller, retreating from an offside position" (Russell Kempson, *The Times*, 10/03/08) put the Baggies 3-1 ahead with 20 minutes remaining and the efficiency of Tony Mowbray's side ultimately proved too strong for The Pirates.

# CIRCUS

WHILE some would wish to point out that watching Rovers week in, week out, was akin to circus entertainment, one Rovers player did join the circus. Jack Kifford, born in Paisley in 1878, joined Rovers from Derby County in 1900 and played in 28 Southern League matches at left-back prior to moving to West Bromwich Albion in June 1901. Later he would represent Millwall, Carlisle United and Coventry City. Having appeared for several clubs, he retired from football in 1909 to join Fred Karno's Troupe. Billy Wragg, who played for Watford when they defeated Rovers 4-0 in a Southern League game in September 1901, was also a performer with the troupe and appeared alongside Charlie Chaplin and Stan Laurel at the London Colisseum, and around the country, in 1910. A solid defender, Wragg had played for a number of clubs, winning an FA Cup-winner's medal in 1898, when he set up the opening goal for Arthur Capes in Nottingham Forest's 3-1 victory over Derby County. Sanger's Circus put on two shows on the pitch at Eastville in June 1922; the company, then 99 years old, performed first at half past two, and then again at eight o'clock in the evening.

# AND THE OLD MAN SCORED

THE only opponent to score against Rovers after his 40th birthday was Arthur Chandler, the celebrated former Leicester City centre-forward, who contributed two of Notts County's six goals in Rovers' demoralisingly heavy defeat at Meadow Lane over Christmas 1935. Mick O'Brien was the oldest opponent to score from the penalty spot against Rovers in the league. Fred Forbes is the oldest former Rovers player to score against the club.

1. Arthur Chandler (Notts Co) ... b. 27/11/95  sc. 28/12/35 ..... 40 years 31 d.
2. Mick O'Brien (Watford) .......... b. 10/08/93  sc. 21/01/33 ... 39 years 164 d.
3. Alan Oakes (Chester) .............. b. 01/09/42  sc. 29/08/81 ... 38 years 353 d.
4. Fred Forbes (Northampton T.) b. 05/08/94  sc. 04/03/33 ... 38 years 211 d.
5. Harry Woods (Luton T.) .......... b. 12/03/90  sc. 06/10/28 ... 38 years 208 d.
6. Gilbert Alsop (Walsall) ............ b. 10/09/08  sc. 26/12/46 ... 38 years 107 d.

## GIANT-KILLINGS

SINCE their elevation to the Football League in 1920, Rovers have defeated several top-division sides. First Division Preston North End lost 2-0 at Eastville in January 1952 thanks to goals from Vic Lambden and Geoff Bradford. Portsmouth were beaten 2-1 at Eastville three years later, with Bradford and Bill Roost scoring for Rovers and John Gordon replying for Pompey. Most famously, the following year, Manchester United's Busby Babes lost 4-0 at Eastville, with Alfie Biggs scoring twice and Barrie Meyer and Bradford grabbing one apiece. Two years later, Burnley were defeated in a replay at Turf Moor, with Welsh forward Dai Ward scoring twice and Norman Sykes once in a 3-2 victory. Jimmy McIlroy and Ray Pointer replied for the home side. In January 1986, First Division Leicester City lost 3-1 at Eastville, when Byron Stevenson scored the opening goal, and Trevor Morgan two more for Rovers, before Gary McAllister replied with a late penalty. In January 2002, the first-ever away FA Cup hat-trick by a Rovers player, Nathan Ellington, earned Rovers a 3-1 win at Derby County, for whom Fabrizio Ravanelli replied. In January 2008 Rovers defeated Fulham at home in a replay, winning 5-3 on penalties after a goalless draw.

## CORNER-KICKS

IT would appear that Tosh Parker is the only Rovers player to have scored direct from a corner in the league. He achieved this feat in scoring the only goal of the game at Swansea in May 1923. Similarly, Watford's veteran forward Tommy Waterall had also scored direct from a corner in Rovers' 2-1 defeat in February 1921. However, as the rules allowing a goal to stand if scored directly from a corner were only introduced in June 1924, some doubt must be thrown on these claims. Brentford's Jackie Foster scored his side's very late winner at Griffin Park in September 1929 direct from a corner. Three players lay claim to having achieved this feat whilst playing for Rovers' reserve side. Roy Davies did so in a 5-1 defeat against Exeter City reserves on Guy Fawkes' Night 1927; Jack Benham managed it in a 1-1 draw with Bristol University in March 1931 after both Chris Hackett and John Richardson had missed penalties; and George Tadman scored directly from two corners in one game, as the reserves defeated their Torquay United counterparts 6-2 at Eastville in October 1933.

# COME FLY WITH ME

CAPTAIN Albert Prince-Cox, Rovers' charismatic manager in the early 1930s, was keen to publicise Rovers as much as possible. In 1932, he chartered a private aeroplane from London to Whitchurch Airport to enable Rovers' influential centre-forward, Vivian Gibbins, a schoolteacher in London during the week, to play in a midweek game at Eastville. Arriving within half an hour of the 6.15 pm kick-off, Gibbins led the attack in a 3-1 victory over Southend United in September 1932. Prince-Cox also flew a group of supporters, at a cost of eight shillings a head, to watch Rovers beat Cardiff City 5-1 at Ninian Park in February 1934. Similar schemes were in place for the trip to Newcastle United in April 1991 and the League Cup tie at Norwich City in September 2004. When Geoff Bradford, then on Rovers' books, played for England against Denmark in Copenhagen in October 1955, the Rovers Supporters' Club chartered a plane for 34 supporters, including Mrs Bradford. Arthur Griffiths, a former Rovers full-back, was in the Notts County side whose 2-0 win against Bristol City in October 1910 was held up by the unexpected fly-past of M. de Lessops in his aeroplane.

# CENTENARY

TO celebrate the club's centenary in 1983, Rovers played three representative matches. First, the club hosted a Spurs side in the spring, losing 3-2 at Eastville. Then, in the centenary week of the club's first fixture, Rovers returned to the scene of the first match on December 4th. Having lost 6-0 to Wotton-under-Edge in December 1883, Rovers defeated Wotton Rovers 4-0, before defeating a representative Newcastle United side 5-4 at Eastville 48 hours later.

# GOALS IN CONSECUTIVE GAMES

THE longest run of consecutive league matches in which Rovers scored was 24 in 1956.

24 league games ..... 10/03/1956 – 20/10/1956
23 league games ..... 16/12/1995 – 13/04/1996
22 league games ..... 17/03/1990 – 03/10/1990
21 league games ..... 12/09/1951 – 07/02/1952

## BALLY'S RECORD

HE may have only appeared in seventeen league games in a Rovers shirt, but World Cup winner Alan Ball is the former Rovers player who has played in the largest number of league matches during his career with many clubs. Ball is joined by two fellow England internationals, Mick Channon and Keith Curle, in having accumulated more than 700 games in the Football League. The league record is 1,005 matches, set by the goalkeeper Peter Shilton, while Rovers manager Paul Trollope's father John made 770 league appearances, all of them in the colours of Swindon Town.

Alan Ball ......................743 ......................................... 17 for Rovers
Mick Channon ............704 + 13 = 717 ................. 4 + 5 for Rovers
Keith Curle ..................675 + 30 = 705 ............. 21 + 11 for Rovers
Geraint Williams..........669 + 5 = 674 ............... 138 + 3 for Rovers
Nigel Martyn...............665 + 1 = 666 ..................... 101 for Rovers
Steve White ................. 547 + 99 = 646 ............. 135 + 15 for Rovers

## PLEADING FOR BAIL

WHEN Rovers travelled to Aldershot for a Third Division (South) fixture in December 1935, an interesting conversation took place in a Hampshire court. The Aldershot chairman was also a well-respected local magistrate and the defendant before him was a Rovers fan. "Please, Sir", he is alleged to have asked. "Can I have bail so that I can go and see the Rovers beat Aldershot?" The request was turned down and Rovers proceded to lose 6-1, then the Shots' largest league victory and still Rovers' heaviest defeat against this opposition. Bert Lutterloch, who scored three goals that day, is the only Aldershot player to have scored a hat-trick against Rovers in competitive football.

## LUXEMBOURG

ONLY one player from Luxembourg has opposed Rovers in the Football League, and he was sent off. Stéphane Gillet, born in August 1977, was in goal for Chester City against Rovers at the Memorial Stadium in January 2007. He conceded two first-half goals and was then sent off for a 70-minute foul on Junior Agogo as Rovers won 2-1.

## FOUR-GOAL PIRATES

JUST as Rovers are unusual in never having scored more than eight goals in a league match, it is equally rare to find a team for whom no player has recorded five or more goals in a game. Several men have scored four times in a league match, with Vic Lambden having achieved this feat on two occasions. Rickie Lambert's four goals at home to Southend United in October 2008 was the first time in almost 50 years that a Rovers player had scored that many in a home league fixture. During Rovers' Southern League years, Jack Jones, Fred Wilcox, John Smith and James Brogan all scored four times in a match, as have Carl Saunders and Paul Miller in FA Cup ties in more recent years. Jack Jones also scored six in an FA Cup tie against Weymouth in 1900, while Bill Weston scored nine as Rovers defeated Great Western Railway 13-0 in a wartime match in February 1917. One Rovers player did score six times in a league match; Tom McCairns, who was with Rovers in the 1898/99 season, scored six goals as Grimsby Town defeated Leicester Fosse in Division Two in April 1896.

Sid Leigh................... 02/05/21................. Rovers 5 Exeter City 0
Jonah Wilcox............. 26/12/25............... Rovers 7 Bournemouth 2
Bill Culley ................ 05/03/27........................... Rovers 4 QPR 1
Frank Curran............. 25/03/39............. Rovers 5 Swindon Town 0
Vic Lambden............. 29/03/48..................... Rovers 7 Aldershot 1
George Petherbridge . 01/12/51............ Rovers 5 Torquay United 0
Vic Lambden............. 14/04/52........ Rovers 6 Colchester United 0
Geoff Bradford .......... 14/03/59....... Rovers 4 Rotherham United 1
Robin Stubbs............. 10/10/70.................. Gillingham 1 Rovers 4
Alan Warboys............ 01/12/73...................... Brighton 2 Rovers 8
Jamie Cureton .......... 16/01/99........................ Reading 0 Rovers 6
Rickie Lambert ......... 25/10/08......... Rovers 4 Southend United 2

## BENIN

THE only Benin international footballer to oppose Rovers was Romuald Boco. Born in the French town of Niort in July 1985, Boco qualified to represent the African nation through his genealogical background and, by November 2009, had won a total of 24 caps, scoring nine goals. The national captain, nicknamed 'The King of Benin', Boco was in the Accrington Stanley side that drew 1-1 with Rovers in a League Two fixture in March 2007.

## HAT-TRICKS FOR FOUR CLUBS

IT is some feat to register a league hat-trick, yet quite something else to score league hat-tricks for as many as four separate clubs. Yet, two former Rovers players have done precisely that. Tom Williams scored all three of Rovers' goals in the club's unlikely 3-2 win away to a resurgent Millwall side in October 1926. He had already scored three times in Gillingham's 6-0 victory over Brentford in March 1924 and was to repeat the feat in Merthyr Town's 5-2 win against Crystal Palace in April 1930 and Norwich City's 4-0 victory against his former club Gillingham eight months later. Steve White also achieved this unlikely feat, scoring the second hat-trick of his professional career in January 1986 when Rovers defeated Darlington 3-1 at Eastville. He was to score two hat-tricks each in the colours of Luton Town (beating Grimsby Town 6-0 in October 1981 and Cambridge United 5-2 in January 1996), and Swindon Town (in a 3-0 victory over Mansfield Town in April 1987 and a 4-0 win at Watford in March 1993). He also scored all the goals as Hereford United defeated Plymouth Argyle 3-0 in April 1996.

## IRISH PLAYER OF THE YEAR

HE may have only spent a brief loan spell with Rovers in 2004/05, but Gary Twigg never scored for the club. However, he gained greater goalscoring fame elsewhere. In a trial game with Derry City in February 2005, he scored five times against Dunboyne and was taken on. Then, over Christmas 2006, Twigg scored a second-half hat-trick as Airdrie United defeated Gretna in a Scottish League match. The 2009 season with Shamrock Rovers in Eire brought Twigg enormous success, though, as his 24 goals left him the top scorer in the league and he was named PFAI Players' Player of the Year.

## NEVER ON A SUNDAY

THE first time Rovers played a Sunday game was in January 1974, when they lost 4-3 away to Nottingham Forest in the FA Cup. The first Sunday Football League match was three weeks later, when Rovers won 3-2 away to Aldershot. Rovers' first home league fixture on a Sunday came in December 1986, when the side drew 2-2 with Newport County at Twerton Park.

## MANAGERS

THE current Rovers manager, Paul Trollope, is the 28th manager of the club since elevation to the Football League in 1920. Of these, only two, Harold Jarman and Ian Holloway, were born in Bristol. Bert Tann was in charge of Rovers for 801 Football League games, significantly more than any other boss. The only Rovers manager to have won a league championship was Malcolm Allison, who led Manchester City to the league title in 1967/68 and managed Rovers in 1992/93. Bobby Gould, twice manager at Eastville, is the only manager who has led a side to an FA Cup Final victory when his Wimbledon side surprised Liverpool 1-0 in 1988. David Williams and Alan Buckley, respectively player-managers of Rovers and Walsall, both scored in Rovers' 4-2 win at Eastville in February 1984. Albert Prince-Cox had refereed several Rovers matches, including the 4-1 win against Crystal Palace in Division Three (South) in April 1927, before becoming manager of the club in November 1930. When Rovers lost 3-1 at Fulham in December 1969 and in both the sides' fixtures the following season, Rovers' manager was Bill Dodgin senior and Fulham were led by his son, Bill Dodgin junior.

## BILLIARDS SALOON

BOTH Sam Irving and Bobby McKay retired from professional football, having played for Rovers during their careers, to set up and run billiards saloons in Scotland. Irving ran a saloon in Dundee, where he was a prominent local character, once donating a set of football shirts to a local club. McKay opened a billiards saloon back in his native Glasgow. They were both teammates at Eastville of athlete Bill Routledge, a wing-half who served Rovers well in the early 1930s and who won the grand sum of £100 from the track; he was excused pre-season training in 1931 so that he could compete in the Powderhall Sprint.

## LAYER ROAD DEBUTANTS

ROVERS had the honour of appearing in the first Football League game played at Layer Road. Colchester United had played in senior non-league football on the ground, but their elevation to the Football League in 1950 brought them into the Third Division (South). Rovers were the first away team there and the sides fought a goalless draw in front of a crowd of 13,687.

## ROVERS GOALS

IN addition to being the only man to have played for England whilst with Rovers, Geoffrey Reginald William Bradford scored more league goals for the club than any other player in Rovers' history. Between 1949 and 1964, he totalled 242 goals in 461 league appearances for his only professional club. Interestingly, no other Rovers player has ever managed as many as 242 league goals when all goals scored with any club are added together; Mick Channon, who never netted for Rovers, contributed a career total of 232, while Steve White's tally of 223 league goals included 44 with Rovers.

| | |
|---|---|
| Geoff Bradford | 242 |
| Alfie Biggs | 178 |
| Harold Jarman | 127 |
| Vic Lambden | 117 |
| Peter Hooper | 101 |
| Bobby Jones | 101 |

## PARIS IN THE SPRING

THE first game played overseas by Rovers came in March 1909, when Rovers took on Southampton under floodlights in Paris in a charity game. The fixture, which finished 5-5, drew a huge amount of interest from the French media, which announced that the clubs offered a 'practical lesson in association football'. One French sports journal published photos of the two sides, both resplendent in stripes, doing battle on foreign turf. Rovers were clearly reliant on goalkeeper Arthur Cartlidge, who made a number of excellent saves. Ahead 2-1 at half-time, Rovers earned a draw through a hat-trick from Fred Corbett, in his third spell with the club, and a goal apiece from Willie Gerrish and Gilbert Ovens.

## PAINTING BY NUMBERS

HAVING suffered a facial injury, Grimsby Town's Stacy Coldicott wore three different numbered shirts in the first nine minutes of Rovers' League Two fixture in February 2005. He started wearing number 11, succumbed to a blood injury and returned wearing number 27, but changed again after just nine minutes, playing out the rest of the match with number 20.

HAROLD JARMAN'S 127 FOOTBALL LEAGUE GOALS INCLUDED THIS ONE AGAINST BRADFORD CITY

## THE BRIEFEST PIRATES

THE shortest league careers for Rovers, in terms of minutes remaining when a player came on to the field as a substitute, are as listed below.

| | | |
|---|---|---|
| 1 min | Louie Soares | 07/05/05 v Wycombe (1m) |
| 3 mins | Scott Sinclair | 26/12/04 v Orient (1m), 9/4/05 v Rushden (2m) |
| 3 mins | Elliott Ward | 15/01/05 v Lincoln (1m), 29/12/04 v. Cheltenham (1m), 03/01/05 v Northampton (1m) |
| 10 mins | David Smith | 24/04/82 v Walsall (10m) |
| 11 mins | Brian Cash | 03/01/05 v Northampton (11m) |
| 14 mins | Anthony Pulis | 09/02/08 v Doncaster R (14m) |
| 17 mins | Wayne Andrews | 29/03/08 v Yeovil (17m from start of match) |
| 21 mins | Ricky Shakes | 26/02/05 v Macclesfield (21m) |
| 22 mins | Charlie Clough | 26/04/08 v Brighton (22m) |
| 25 mins | Darren Mullings | 31/12/05 v Wycombe (18m), 21/01/06 v Chester (5m), 04/02/06 v Bury (1m), 11/03/06 v Notts Co (1m) |
| 26 mins | David Byrne | 10/02/90 v. Preston (18m), 18/02/90 v Walsall (8m) |
| 27 mins | Mick Adams | 14/05/83 v. Cardiff (27m) |
| 30 mins | Alan Routledge | 17/01/81 v. Grimsby (30m) |
| 32 mins | Jason Eaton | 15/08/87 v. Rotherham (5m), 28/12/87 v Southend (25m), 16/01/88 v Northampton (2m) |
| 36 mins | Graham Barrett | 16/12/00 v. Stoke (36m) |
| 38 mins | Billy Foreman | 08/03/77 v. Blackburn (26m), 04/04/78 v. Oldham (12m) |

## FLOODLIGHTS

ROVERS' first home game under floodlights was an evening Second Division encounter against Ipswich Town in September 1959. A crowd of 24,093 saw Peter Hooper's two goals earn Rovers a 2-1 victory, with Ted Phillips replying for the visitors. Rovers were the visitors at Millmoor when Rotherham United played their first floodlit home fixture. The League Cup third-round game in November 1960 drew a crowd of 10,912 and United won 2-0, with Ken Houghton and Alan Kirkman scoring their goals.

## SENT OFF AGAINST YOUR CLUB

IT is unusual to be sent off while playing against a club you also appeared for, but five ex-Rovers players have received red cards in league action against Rovers, whilst playing in the colours of another club. Four of these occasions were when Rovers were playing a club whose name begins with a 'W', whilst three occasions came against Welsh clubs. Llewellyn's red card in north Wales came at a time when he had scored the only goal of the game.

Larry Lloyd (Wigan Athletic)..... 16/10/82 ....Rovers 4 Wigan Athletic 0
Carl Heggs (Swansea City).......... 19/08/95 ........ Rovers 2 Swansea City 2
Andy Rammell (Wycombe W.) .. 12/09/00 ........Wycombe W. 0 Rovers 1
Danny Williams (Wrexham)....... 05/05/01 .............. Rovers 4 Wrexham 0
Chris Llewellyn (Wrexham) ....... 28/10/06 .............. Wrexham 2 Rovers 0

## DISASTER FUND

IN May 1912, Rovers lost 3-1 to Bristol City in a match to raise money for the Titanic Disaster Fund. Before a crowd of 1,500, Rovers took the lead five minutes before half-time through Bill Hurley only to lose the game after the interval. Similarly, in May 1946, the clubs met to raise funds for the Bolton Disaster Fund, following the catastrophic events at Bolton's Burnden Park ground in which 33 people died. Before a crowd of 9,859, Rovers conceded six second-half goals to lose 7-1, with inside-right Doug Baldie contributing the consolation goal.

## ENGLAND PLAYER LODGING

KEN Boyes played just twice for Rovers, as an outside-left in the 1922/23 season, between stints at Southampton and Weymouth. Born in Southampton in November 1895, he died in Eastleigh in October 1963. Boyes came from a sporting background, his brother Stuart playing 474 times for Hampshire County Cricket Club. The three Boyes brothers were heavily influenced by sport from a young age. The 1901 census reveals that their home in Milton Road, Shirley was also home to a lodger, the England international footballer Arthur Chadwick.

## WELSH CUP

ROVERS entered the Welsh Cup in 1932/33 and 1933/34, playing a total of four matches, of which one was won and two lost, Rovers' six goals each being scored by different players. Alec Donald played in all these fixtures. The highest attendance at any Rovers game was 3,500 for the 3-0 defeat at Swansea in February 1933. Rovers scored twice in a minute against Port Vale in March 1934, a game that finished 3-3. Bristol City won the Welsh Cup in 1933/34, one of six seasons in which they competed, with former Rovers striker Joe Riley scoring two goals in the final. Other Rovers players have played in Welsh Cup finals; Jason Perry (four), Jack Evans three with Cardiff City, Paul Raynor scoring in two finals with Swansea City, and others playing once each: Sid Homer (Bristol City), Joe Clennell, Bryn Jones and Nicky Platnauer (Cardiff City), Idris Lewis (Newport County), Ashley Griffiths, Tom Ramasut and Jon French (Barry Town), George Crisp (Merthyr Town), Terry Oldfield (Wrexham) and George Millington (Shrewsbury Town) amongst them.

## MARRIED FIRST

JOHN Stapleton was married on the morning of March 1st 1958. That afternoon, he was in the Fulham side that played Rovers in an FA Cup quarter-final, only the second of three occasions that Rovers have reached this stage of the tournament. Despite a goal from Geoff Bradford, Rovers lost 3-1 at Craven Cottage to go out of the cup. Born in June 1928, Stapleton was a tough centre-half who played for Fulham, his only professional club, in 97 league games during the 1950s, scoring twice.

## THE 'SON OF GOD'

THE broadcaster David Icke, who famously declared himself the 'Son of God', made his senior footballing debut against Rovers. Born in Leicester in May 1952, he joined Hereford United from Coventry City in August 1971 and first played for The Bulls in a pre-season friendly against Rovers at Edgar Street later that month. The sides drew 1-1 after Mike Green had given Rovers the lead five minutes before half-time. Icke saved well from Wayne Jones and Sandy Allan, who also hit a post, before Billy Meadows equalised nine minutes from time. Icke never played against Rovers in league football.

## SOME FAMOUS OPPONENTS

MANY celebrated footballers have opposed Rovers down the years – George Best, Bobby Charlton, Tom Finney and Brian Clough are four such examples. C. B. Fry, who played for England at football and cricket, played in the 1902 FA Cup Final, held the world long jump record, stood for parliament and famously declined the Kingship of Albania, played for Portsmouth against Rovers in January 1903. Herbert Chapman, the highly successful inter-war manager at both Huddersfield Town and Arsenal, played for Sheppey United against Rovers in a Southern League game in December 1899. Manager Jock Stein was in the non-league Llanelli side that Rovers knocked out of the FA Cup in 1950/51. Harold Halse, a forward who played for three different sides in FA Cup finals and scored six goals in the 1911 Charity Shield, played for Charlton Athletic against Rovers in 1921/22. Gary Lineker scored for Leicester City reserves against Rovers reserves in November 1983. Lior David, a nephew of Uri Geller, scored twice for Swansea City reserves against Rovers reserves in September 1998.

## ROVERS PLAYING CRICKET

IN August 1936, Rovers defeated Bristol City at cricket by fifteen runs. Rovers were fortunate to have two decent opening batsmen in Allan Murray and the Somerset cricketer Newman Bunce, scoring 227 runs and taking four wickets. Sixteen years later, in September 1952, the former Rovers full-back Charles Littlewood organised a cricket match between Rovers and the Duke of Beaufort's XI. Littlewood top-scored for the Duke's side with 26 runs as his side ran up a total of 164 all out. Rovers scored 75-5 in reply, with Ronnie Dix ending as top scorer with 23.

## PLAY-OFFS

ROVERS have played in four sets of play-off fixtures, attempting to get out of the third tier of English football in 1988/89, 1994/95 and 1997/98 and out of the fourth tier in 2006/07. Rovers lost a Wembley final to Huddersfield Town in 1995 and defeated Shrewsbury Town at Wembley in 2007 to seal promotion. In all, Rovers have played in 12 play-off matches, winning six of them and scoring 21 goals in the process. Richard Walker has scored four goals in play-off matches, more than any other Rovers player.

## TWO GOALS EACH

THREE opponents have scored two goals each against Rovers on five occasions in the Football League. Most of these occasions were to end in demoralising defeats. Against Brighton, Frank Curran scored twice for Rovers, so this is the only time that four separate players have each scored two goals in a league match involving Rovers.

28/12/31 ...Northampton Town 6 Rovers 0 .................................................
.................................................*Ted Bowen 2, Harry Lovatt 2, Tommy Wells 2*
13/02/32 ...Norwich City 6 Rovers 0 .......................................................
................................................. *Oliver Brown 2, Cyril Blakemore 2, Sam Bell 2*
29/04/39 ...Brighton 6 Rovers 3 .............................................................
.................................................*Herbert Goffey 2, Herbert Stephens 2, Robert Farrell 2*
25/12/56 ...Bury 7 Rovers 2 ..................................................................
................................................. *Stan Pearson 3, Tom Neill 2, Eddie Robertson 2*
19/01/57 ...Leicester City 7 Rovers 2 ......................................................
*Tommy McDonald 2, Arthur Rowley 2 (1 pen), Billy Wright 2, Derek Hines*

## THE COCOA MAKER

BORN in Bristol in the autumn of 1878, Harry Bennett was to appear in one Southern League game for Rovers, a 2-0 defeat at West Ham United in April 1906 when he played at outside-left. He is listed on the 1901 census as a 'cocoa maker', living at home in Ernestville Road, Fishponds with his widowed mother Matilda and his younger sister Maud. Indeed, the cocoa maker signed for Rovers in 1905 after playing for Frys Athletic, the works team. He joined Fishponds United in 1906.

## EURO 2008

COLIN Kazim-Richards, who played for Bury against Rovers, was in the Turkey side that reached the semi-finals of Euro 2008. Whilst, out of Rovers players, only Alan Ball has played in a European championship semi-final, nine league opponents have done so. Six of England's 1968 squad, two of England's 1996 team and Kazim-Richards have all achieved this feat. A further eight players – five from 1968 and three from 1996 – opposed Rovers in cup football but never in the league.

## LEAGUE CHAMPIONS

THE following Rovers players appeared for the league champions in England during their careers. Bobby McKay played for both Scottish champions Rangers and English champions Newcastle United in the 1926/27 season.

Jack Allen......... Sheffield Wednesday ........................1928/29, 1929/30
Alan Ball.......... Everton ............................................................... 1969/70
Cliff Britton..... Everton ............................................................... 1938/39
Larry Lloyd...... Liverpool, Nottm Forest....................1972/73, 1977/78
Terry Cooper .. Leeds United ...................................................... 1968/69
Bobby McKay . Newcastle United .............................................. 1926/27
David Steele .... Huddersfield Town............ 1922/23, 1923/24, 1924/25
Phil Taylor ....... Liverpool............................................................ 1946/47
Joe Walter ........ Huddersfield Town.............................1923/24, 1924/25

## AGGREGATE GOALS IN A SEASON

THE highest number of goals that Rovers have recorded against any other league club in a season is ten. During the 1956/57 season, Rovers won 4-2 at Doncaster Rovers and then defeated the same opposition 6-1 at Eastville. This feat was repeated in the 1998/99 season when Rovers, having defeated Reading 4-1 early in the campaign, won 6-0 at the Madejski Stadium, with Jamie Cureton registering the first four goals. On the other hand, the greatest number of goals conceded by Rovers against one side in a league campaign was 14. Having drawn 2-2 with Luton Town at Eastville in 1935/36, Rovers capitulated to a disastrous 12-0 defeat at Kenilworth Road.

## A HOLE IN ONE

CHARLES Preedy, who played in goal in 39 league games for Rovers in the mid-1930s, hit a hole-in-one at the eighth hole on Knowle Golf Course in 1934. He also played for Arsenal in the 1930 FA Cup Final against Huddersfield Town. Rovers' club captain in 1928, Jack Cosgrove, entered the British Amateur Open championship in 1930, the year that he left Eastville, and had limited success for several years thereafter.

## THREE PENALTIES IN A MATCH

ON five occasions in league matches featuring Rovers, there have been as many as three penalties awarded. Twice, all three were converted. Wing-half Jackie Pitt scored twice for Rovers and Len Emmanuel once for Newport County in the game at Eastville in March 1948; John Mackin scored twice for York City and Harold Jarman once for Rovers in the match at Eastville in October 1971. In December 1928, wing-half Albert Rotherham and forward Jack Phillips both missed penalties for Rovers, whilst Swindon Town's Walter Dickinson scored from the rebound after his kick had been saved. After George McNestry's penalty had given Rovers a half-time lead, Gillingham's Dick Doncaster and Joe Wiggins both missed second-half penalties in May 1935. In March 1937, Harold 'Happy' Houghton scored one of two penalties awarded in Rovers' favour at Ninian Park, whilst Cardiff City's Arthur Granville scored from the spot. Apart from the Swindon game, both sides are known to have missed penalties at Eastville in March 1958, Rovers' Peter Hooper and Orient's John Hartburn in Rovers' 4-0 win.

## THREE DECADES

NINE individual players have appeared for Rovers in competitive football in three separate decades during their careers. The first was Harry Horsey, whose first known appearance, in the days before comprehensive records, came in a goalless draw with Warmley in November 1884. He last played for Rovers in March 1900. Jesse Whatley played his first game for the club in November 1919 and made his final Football League appearance in May 1930. Since World War II seven more celebrated Rovers names have also achieved the feat: Geoff Bradford, Harold Jarman, Bobby Jones, George Petherbridge, Frankie Prince, Stuart Taylor and Ray Warren.

## MASSACRES

JAMES Durkan, who played for Rovers in two league fixtures in 1935, was born in July 1915 at Bannockburn, the place where King Edward II had been defeated and repelled by Robert the Bruce in 1314. Donnie Gillies, a Bristol City stalwart who enjoyed two seasons with Rovers in the early 1980s in the twilight of his career, was born in June 1951 at Glencoe, where the Campbells instigated a celebrated massacre in February 1692.

## JASON ROBERTS MBE

JASON Roberts, who was with Rovers from 1998 until his transfer to West Bromwich Albion in 2000 – scoring 38 goals in 73 (plus five as substitute) league matches – earned rave reviews in the press. He was "like a Pamplona bull"(Stuart Hall, February 2005); he was "the shape and size of a brick out-house, full of honest industry and a man who takes no nonsense from anyone"(Roy Collins, *The Sunday Telegraph*, January 2006). Roberts was awarded an MBE in the 2010 New Year's Honours List for his services to charity in supporting sport for young people. He soon linked up at Rovers with Nathan 'The Duke' Ellington, who was the reigning Surrey county high-jump champion when he joined Rovers in February 1999 and also competed in county trials at long jump, 100m and 200m. Ellington played in 76 (plus 40 as substitute) league games for Rovers, scoring 35 times. "He's a jigsaw puzzle," said Gary Penrice of 'The Duke', "all the pieces are there, it's just a matter of putting them together."

## FIRST TIME OUT

ROVERS' first-ever game finished in a 6-0 defeat at Wotton-under-Edge in December 1883. The game was scarcely mentioned in the local press and all that remains for the modern supporter is a scoreline. However, based on line-ups for later that season, it is likely that founder members Bill Braund, Fred Channing, Richard Conyers, Henry Martin and the Horsey brothers, Harry and Bob, would all have featured in the match. It is possible that Bill Small could have played in goal, with the rest of the side perhaps being Lewis Davies, Fred Hall, Bill Pepperell and George Warne.

## GUINNESS BOOK OF RECORDS

ONE Rovers player whose name appears regularly in the *Guinness Book of Records* is Jimmy Smith. A Rovers player between 1933 and 1935, he had previously scored 72 domestic goals for Ayr United in the 1927/28 season, a tally which included 66 in the Scottish Second Division. This astonishing British seasonal goalscoring record is unlikely ever to be surpassed. Born in Old Kilpatrick in March 1902, Smith joined Rovers from Tunbridge Wells Rangers and his 13 goals in 26 league appearances included two hat-tricks. He died in Connecticut in 1975.

## THE MAGIC OF THE FA CUP

GEORGE Petherbridge played for Rovers in 40 FA Cup ties, more than any other player at the club. Geoff Bradford and Stuart Taylor played in 38 each. Vic Lambden scored 16 goals in the tournament in his career, with Bradford totalling 15 and Alfie Biggs 13. Jason Roberts' seven goals in the competition proper in 1998/99 is a club seasonal best and won him the coveted FA Cup Golden Boot award that season. Prior to Football League status in 1920, Jack Jones had scored six times in a 15-1 win against Weymouth in November 1900 and five goals 12 months later against the same long-suffering opposition; these fixtures were in qualifying games and not in the competition proper. Carl Saunders, against Plymouth Argyle in January 1992, and Paul Miller, against Bath City in November 1994, both scored four times in an FA Cup tie, whilst Nathan Ellington's hat-trick at top flight Derby County in January 2002 was the first-ever in the FA Cup by a Rovers player away from home.

## EXTRA TIME

WHEN Rovers played away to Aberdare Athletic in a Third Division (South) fixture in February 1923, the game finished by mistake five minutes early. Once the referee's error had been pointed out to him by a linesman, the players returned to play out the remaining time – the match finished goalless. Rovers featured in six league fixtures at Aberdare's Athletic Ground, following the Welsh club's elevation to the Football League in 1921. In 1927, having finished bottom of the division, seven points adrift of Watford, Athletic failed to be re-elected to the league and were replaced by Torquay United.

## CHARABANC

AS was often the norm in the inter-war years, Rovers travelled to Brentford by charabanc for the Third Division (South) fixture of September 1929. En route, though, the vehicle hit an electric standard and three windows were smashed. Fortunately, there were no injuries and the team continued on their journey. Despite leading with ten minutes left through a Jack Phillips goal, Rovers lost 2-1 to late strikes from Jackie Foster and Bill Lane. The Bees went on to win all 21 of their home league fixtures that season, though Rovers had arguably run them the closest.

## ALBERT IN GOAL

ALBERT Boyce played in goal for Rovers in both the Birmingham League and the Southern League. Born in March 1875 in Bristol, he lived in Grafton Street with his widowed mother Maria and two younger brothers. The oldest of six, he had seen his three younger sisters, Lucy, Sarah and Lilly, move away from home in search of work. His father George, a labourer from Stoke Gifford, had died prior to Albert's Rovers debut. A goalkeeper of some merit, he broke into the side in the 1898/99 season, the club's final Birmingham League campaign, and appeared in two fixtures that year. Once the club was promoted to the Southern League over the summer of 1899, he was to play in one game in the new league the following season. Albert Boyce married Mary Elizabeth Bennett in Bristol on Christmas Day 1908 and continued to live in the city, dying in the autumn of 1936 at the age of 52.

## LEICESTER'S FIRST GOAL

THE only child of Scotsman Robert Douglas and his wife Margaret MacKie, George Douglas, born in Stepney in 1893, was a member of the West Ham United side that won the English Schools Shield in 1906/07 and went on to score five times from outside-right in 45 league appearances for Rovers between 1926 and 1928. He also played for Leicester City, Burnley and Oldham Athletic, scoring the first goal that Leicester ever registered in the Football League. In wartime football, he played in six countries before appearing in court for desertion of his wife; the case collapsed. An experienced footballer, George Douglas died in Southborough, Kent in January 1979.

## FOOTBALL LEAGUE XI

SEVEN players who have appeared for Rovers during their career also played for a Football League XI. Cliff Britton and Phil Taylor both played on four occasions, Joe Clennell three times between the wars, and Alan Ball, Mick Channon, Peter Hooper and Marcus Stewart once each. In addition, Bill Culley played for the Scottish League, Joe Walter represented the Southern League and Jesse Whatley played for the South against the North in an England trial game. Harry Bamford, Bill Hartill, Jack Hills and Harold Houghton all represented a Football Association XI.

## HIGH FIVES

WHEN Rovers defeated Portsmouth 5-1 in Division Three at Eastville in November 1982, the goals were scored by players in consecutively numbered shirts – Tim Parkin (5), Aiden McCaffrey (6), Ian Holloway (7), David Williams (8) and Archie Stephens (9). All five members of West Ham United's forward line scored when they defeated Rovers 5-2 at Upton Park in September 1954. John Evans scored all of Liverpool's goals when they won 5-3 against Rovers at Anfield later the same month. Rovers have twice scored exactly five goals in consecutive league matches and have also lost two consecutive matches conceding five goals twice. All five league games Rovers played in February 1995 were away from home. On seven occasions a Rovers player has scored five league goals in one season against the same opposition – the most recent being Rickie Lambert against Hereford United in 2008/09.

## AMATEUR SCORERS

ONLY three amateurs have ended a league campaign as their club's top goalscorer. Charles Mortimore achieved this feat with 15 goals for Aldershot in Division Three (South) in 1949/50 as did George Bromilow for Southport in the Northern section with 22 goals in 1955/56 and eight the following campaign. The third player was Viv Gibbins who, not content with his 18-goal haul for West Ham United in Division One in 1930/31, performed a similar feat for Rovers in 1932/33. He scored 14 goals that season to finish as Rovers' top goalscorer with four more than Billy Jackson. Gibbins scored 15 goals in 37 league appearances for Rovers; he was later headmaster of Harold Road School in West Ham.

## QUICK-FIRE JULES

JULIAN Alsop, who scored just four times in over thirty league appearances for Rovers in the late 1990s, was the recognised scorer of a two-minute hat-trick. His three goals for Tamworth Town against Armitage in a Beazer Homes League Southern Division match in 1994/95 were timed as 11, 11 and 13 minutes. Five years later, he almost repeated the feat, when he scored a hat-trick in four minutes in Swansea City's 7-0 win against Cwmbran Town in a Welsh Premier Cup match. This remains the fastest hat-trick registered by a Swansea player.

ARCHIE STEPHENS SCORED ONE OF ROVERS' FIVE GOALS AGAINST POMPEY IN 1982

## FA CUP NIGHTMARES

IT is a fate that befalls every league club, but Rovers have been knocked out of the FA Cup by a non-league side on five occasions since the club's elevation to the Football League in 1920. In November 1946, Merthyr Tydfil defeated Rovers 3-1 with Bill Hullett scoring twice and George Crisp, a pre-war Rovers player, also finding the net; Vic Lambden replied for Rovers. Bobby Hatt's goal in November 1972 gave Hayes a 1-0 victory over the Pirates. Despite an Andy Reece goal, Rovers then lost 2-1 at Kettering Town in December 1988, with Robbie Cooke scoring twice for the Northamptonshire club. In November 1995, Rovers suffered a humiliating 2-1 defeat at Hitchin Town, whose goals came from Steve Conroy and Lee Burns, Lee Archer pulling a goal back for Rovers. Finally, during their brief exile from the league, Carlisle United defeated Rovers 1-0 through Magno Vieira's goal in November 2004.

## FOILED BY THE WHISTLE

AS a home game with Orient moved into the final stages, Rovers went all-out for the late winning goal. John Rudge was brought on as substitute as Rovers tried a three-man attack at the close of this Second Division game in November 1974. In the dying seconds, a corner was won on the right at the Muller Road End of the old ground at Eastville. Gordon Fearnley ran across to take the kick and his cross was met by the head of Rudge and powered into the net. A deafening cheer resounded from previously despairing voices in the Tote End. Sadly, for all those attached to Rovers, the referee had blown the final whistle as the corner came across, so the 'goal' was disallowed and the match remained scoreless.

## DIRECTOR'S DAUGHTER

WILLIAM Mark Hasell, born in Clifton in 1873, was a Rovers director who served the club until resigning through ill health in September 1930. His daughter met George Barton, a Rovers player from 1928 to 1931 and the couple got married in 1932, with Barton's former Rovers teammate Fred Forbes acting as best man. Jimmy Watson, who played for Rovers in 1933/34, joined the club from Tunbridge Wells Rangers, where he had met his wife Mary, the daughter of a Tunbridge director.

## THREE SPELLS

WHEN he played as player-manager against Peterborough United in August 1996, Ian Holloway became the first player to have represented Rovers in league football in three separate spells with the club. Having made his debut against Wrexham in April 1981, Holloway enjoyed three spells with Rovers between 1981 and 1985, 1987 and 1991 and 1996 and 1999, playing in 379 league games and scoring 42 goals. Two other players, though, have appeared for the club in three separate stints. Fred Corbett played Southern League football for Rovers in three different spells between 1902 and 1903, in 1905 and from 1908 to 1911, scoring 52 times in 139 appearances. Likewise, 'Tot' Farnall also represented Rovers in three different spells with the club. He was briefly with Rovers in the Birmingham and District League in 1895 and from 1897 to 1899, before playing 20 times in the Southern league with the club between 1901 and 1903.

## PROMOTION

ROVERS have been promoted four times during their time in the Football League. The club moved up from third-tier football in 1952/53, 1973/74 and 1989/90 and from fourth-tier football in 2006/07. In 1952/53 and 1989/90 Rovers completed the season as champions of their division. Tony Sealy, who played in Rovers' 1989/90 season, held an astonishing record of having won four championship medals with four different clubs in the space of a decade; he was with Queens Park Rangers (1982/83), AFC Bournemouth (1986/87), Rovers (1989/90) and Brentford (1991/92). Bob Anderson was the only player to appear in championship-winning sides in the same division with two clubs from the same city; he played for Rovers (1952/53) and Bristol City (1954/55).

## HOT FUZZ

THERE had been reported sightings of Rovers shirts in episodes of *EastEnders* and *Auf Wiedersehen Pet*, but Rovers' distinctive quarters, complete with their logo for sponsors Cowlin Construction made their film bow in *Hot Fuzz*, when actor Nick Frost, a self-professed West Ham United fan, acting the part of Danny Butterman, appeared in several scenes sporting the shirt. Rovers fans leapt on this as a sign of some allegiance to the club, but at least the 2007 blockbuster film brought a degree of fame to the quartered top.

# THE TOMMY COOK STORY

THE annals of Brighton & Hove Albion Football Club list centre-forward Thomas Edwin Reed Cook as the club's all-time top goalscorer with 113 goals in 190 league games. Yet, Cook's career was more than that: an England cap in 1925, a stint as Rovers' top scorer in 1931/32 with 18 league goals, a football career ended by a broken collarbone playing for Rovers against Cardiff City in January 1933, cricket for Sussex including a score of 278 against Hampshire at Hove in 1930, topping the county averages in 1933, an aviator in the South African Air Force, the sole survivor of an air crash in 1947, Brighton manager later that year, and finally suicide in 1950, at the age of just 49. Cook played in 42 league games for Rovers, scoring 20 times, as a replacement for the Eastville favourite Arthur Attwood, who himself ended up at the Goldstone Ground.

# DON REVIE'S FATHER-IN-LAW

THOMAS Grossett Duncan, known to one and all as 'Tom', scored twice for Rovers in 13 league games in the 1926/27 season, when he competed with Hugh Adcock for the position of outside-right. Born in Lochgelly, Scotland in September 1897, he also played for Leicester City and Halifax Town, having made his name in Scottish football with Raith Rovers. His brother John 'Tokey' Duncan was a Scottish international who once scored six goals for Leicester City in a league game against Port Vale on Christmas Day 1924. Having died in February 1940, Tom Duncan was posthumously the father-in-law of England manager Don Revie as – after Duncan's death – his daughter Elsie married the Leeds United manager. Elsie Revie died in Edinburgh in March 2005, aged 77.

# NORWEGIAN CUP FINAL

WHICH Rovers player appeared in the Norwegian Cup Final of 2005? The answer is the Swedish defender of Liberian extraction, Marcus Andreasson, whose two spells with Rovers included scoring the first of three first-half goals in a 3-1 win at Swindon Town in October 2000. There was talk of a potential international call-up but, though that never materialised, he was to enjoy a long career first with Bryne FK and later with Molde, for whom he played in the 2005 final, which was won 4-2 against Lillestrom.

# THE MEM

THE unofficial Cambridge United website 'Moosenet' reported in January 2005 that Rovers possessed "a frankly lacklustre side... talks of a promotion push resemble a Pukka Pie in the sky on this mediocre evidence". The wordsmith involved continued to describe the stadium where his side had played, describing "its quaint architecture unique in that it boasts one stand that would look more at home at Newmarket Racecourse (and) one temporary effort... more suited to polo". However, the idea of a new stadium remains unpopular with some local residents as well as certain people on a national level, whilst various pressure groups continue to exert a degree of pressure. In February 2007, as enthusiasm grew for the building of new stadia to house the 2018 Olympics, *The Observer* newspaper published a letter from John Hart of Sunderland who opposed "building a new national stadium for a couple of thousand Bristol Rovers fans and some rugby-loving farmers out of geographical tokenism".

# ZENITH DATA SYSTEMS CUP

FOLLOWING promotion to Division Two in 1990, Rovers competed in this tournament for all Second Division clubs in two consecutive seasons until 1992. Rovers beat Watford 2-1, lost 2-1 to Crystal Palace and lost 3-1 at home to Ipswich Town; Tony Pounder, one of eight players to appear in all three games, scored two of the club's four goals. Palace won the 1990/91 final, while the former Rovers defender Kevin Moore scored at Wembley in the 1991/92 final, though his Southampton side lost 3-2 to Nottingham Forest. Two former Rovers players won winners' medals in this competition, Keith Curle with Reading in 1988 and Nigel Martyn with Crystal Palace in 1991.

# THREE IN A ROW

IN both Rovers' fixtures against Queens Park Rangers in the 1922/23 season, the side lost 3-1; in both games, Dick Parker, Arthur Chandler and Arthur Davis scored a goal apiece for Rangers. Rovers conceded exactly six goals at Craven Cottage in three consecutive seasons, losing 6-1 in 1928/29 and 6-2 in 1929/30 and 1930/31. In each of Mark Smith's first three league appearances for Rovers, the Pirates were reduced to nine men, having had two men sent off; Smith never received a red card in his time with Rovers.

# RE-ELECTION

FOR many years, the clubs finishing the season at the foot of the Football League had to apply for re-election. This meant relying on fellow members of the league to vote in your favour. Rovers had to apply on one occasion. In April 1939, Rovers completed their season by losing 6-3 at Brighton & Hove Albion to drop into the bottom two. On the same afternoon, Orient beat Swindon Town 5-0 and they later drew a rescheduled fixture to move clear of trouble, whilst Walsall beat Cardiff City 6-3 to move off bottom place. So, Rovers and Walsall were left on 33 points each to apply for re-election, with Orient safe on 35. Rovers received 45 votes from other clubs and Walsall 36, so both were re-elected. Gillingham, who had left the league twelve months earlier, gained fifteen votes, while Chelmsford City and Colchester United got one each.

# PIONEERING KNEE SURGERY

JAMIE Shore played in midfield for Rovers in eighteen (plus six more as substitute) league matches in the 1998/99 season. A player of unquestionable talent, he had picked up a knee injury in the first thirty seconds of a youth game for Norwich City against Arsenal that had kept him out of the game for 22 months. He underwent pioneering surgery in 1999 with Dr Angus Stover in London, which involved taking cartilage from a dead body, and spent £7,000 on further treatment in Florida in December 2000 with John Barrett. Unfortunately for Shore, his playing career was over, though his voice is still heard on local radio sports commentary.

# INTERNATIONAL RED CARD

THE only player who has appeared for Rovers in league football, and been sent off in an international match, was Alan Ball. The diminutive midfielder, who ended his illustrious career with seventeen league games for Rovers in 1983, was also the holder of 72 England caps as well as a World Cup winner's medal in 1966. A midfield dynamo with a shock of curly red hair, Ball was a distinctive figure. He was sent off during England under-23's goalless draw with Austria in Vienna in June 1965 and received his marching orders in Chorzow in June 1973, when England lost a World Cup qualifying match 2-0 to Poland.

## YOUNGEST GOALSCORING OPPONENTS

NOT content with holding the record as Rovers' youngest league opponent, Notts County's Bob Woolley scored against Rovers over Easter 1964 to become the youngest player to register a league goal against the club. Woolley scored just two goals in nine matches with County, his only league club, and died in 1971, aged 33. Cliff Bastin and Ricky Hill were destined to play for England.

1. Bob Woolley (Notts County)............b. 29/12/47 sc. 09/04/64...16 years 102 d.
2. Edward Davis (Southend United) ...b. 21/05/22 sc. 14/01/39...16 years 210 d.
3. Alick Jeffrey (Doncaster Rovers) ......b. 29/01/39 sc. 24/12/55...16 years 329 d.
4. Cliff Bastin (Exeter City)...................b. 14/03/12 sc. 30/03/29.....17 years 16 d.
5. Ricky Hill (Luton Town) (sub).........b. 05/03/59 sc. 19/04/76.....17 years 44 d.

## FAMOUS BIRTHDAY

BACK in December 1969, the world's greatest player – Pelé – strode forward to take a penalty. When he calmly converted the spot kick, he revealed a T-shirt under his top bearing the figure 1,000; he had become the first player in the world to score 1,000 first-class goals. On the same day, David Hillier was born in Blackheath. "A proper homegrown star" (*The Observer*, May 2008), Hillier won a league championship medal with Arsenal in 1990/91 and also played for Portsmouth before spending three seasons with Rovers between 1999 and a 2002 move to Barnet. He played for Rovers in 82 (plus one as substitute) league matches, scoring one goal.

## TEAM SELECTION

ROVERS used only seventeen players in 46 league matches in 1983/84, and as many as thirty in 1996/97. Rovers made six changes to their league side on six occasions between the wars and on one post-war occasion, following a 3-0 defeat at home to Northampton Town in November 1946. Following their 7-1 defeat at Eastville in January 1935, Northampton Town made nine changes, two of them positional, to their side. Rovers fielded an unchanged side in twelve consecutive league matches in their first post-war season, winning eight and losing two of these fixtures.

# ROVERS RESERVES

EVERYONE knows that there are only two football teams in Bristol: Rovers and Rovers reserves! The reserves played in Division Two of the Western League from 1893/94 to 1896/97 and between 1901/02 and 1908/09. During these final eight seasons, the reserves never finished outside the top five and were champions on three occasions; 1902/03, 1904/05 and 1905/06. During the 1904/05 season, Rovers were unbeaten, yet only pipped Bristol City on goal average, having scored 76 goals and conceded five in sixteen fixtures. The following season Rovers scored 90 goals in eighteen games to retain the title. The reserves then played in Division One of the Western League from 1909/10 to 1913/14 (finishing as champions in 1912/13) from 1919/20 to 1920/21 and 1925/26 to 1947/48. They were champions again in 1928/29, 1935/36, 1936/37 and the first post-war season, 1945/46, when they scored an impressive 120 goals in 26 games. In addition, a side was entered in the Birmingham and District League for 1899/1900 and again for 1936/37, when they were champions with 127 goals in 36 matches. Withdrawing very late from the 1937/38 season, Rovers incurred a £50 fine and became the only champions of that league not to retain their title. They also played in the Southern League from 1920/21 to 1938/39 and in various divisions of the Football Combination from 1946/47, finishing second in 1954/55 and ending up as Second Division champions in 1992/93. Some impressive victories included 12-1 against Cheltenham Town in January 1934, 12-1 against Trowbridge Town in September 1906, 11-0 against Paulton Rovers in December 1914, 10-1 against Ebbw Vale in January 1931, 10-3 against Weymouth in December 1925, 12-2 against a Monmouthshire Senior League XI in January 1937 and 18-2, having led 11-2 at half-time, against HMS Antelope in November 1904, with Fred Latham and Walter Gerrish scoring six apiece. Rovers reserves defeated Portsmouth 9-1 both in January 1952 and in January 1959. In other high-scoring games, the reserves lost 7-5 to both Torquay United reserves in September 1930 and Swindon Town four months later, and beat a Newport League XI 8-6 in March 1930 and Crystal Palace reserves 6-5 in August 1975. Conversely, the side lost 10-1 at Llanelli in November 1932, having conceded six first-half goals, and trailed 8-0 at half-time before losing 9-0 to Spurs in October 1997. The following month Colin Cramb scored all six goals as Rovers reserves lost 6-0 to Bristol City. Harry Poulter scored six goals as Exeter City beat Rovers reserves 9-3 in December 1932.

# PROFESSIONS

IN addition to the usual array of football coaches and publicans, several Rovers players have held down unusual jobs. William Hall, who played in the 1905/06 season, was a steeplejack, Samuel Rinder, a goalkeeper in 1888/89, was an ostrich feather manufacturer and James Vernon (1887/88) was a shearing machine minder. Edward Tucker (1883-91) and William Small (1883/84) both worked as coach painters, whilst Bill Taylor (1887-93) was a French polisher. John Rumens (1891/92) was a boot maker's clicker, Peter O'Grady (1896-99) was a slaughter butcher, James McEwan (1895-97) was a paper maker, Tom Haycock (1893/94) was a railway carriage wood turner and John Earles (1887/88) was a packer at a biscuit factory. Levi Draycott (1900/01) worked as a potter's hollow presser, Albert Cowlin (1884/85) was a 'galvanise labourer' and Fred Bartlett (1893/94) was an organ builder's apprentice. Hubert Ashton (1924/25) was a Conservative Member of Parliament and Fred Hodgkinson (1883/84) was a clergyman.

# ROVERS 4 MANCHESTER UNITED 0

THE Busby Babes arrived at Eastville in January 1956 for an FA Cup third round fixture described in the *Bristol Evening Post* as 'Rovers' finest hour'. Though Duncan Edwards was missing through injury, the full strength United side featured five players who were tragically to lose their lives two years later in the Munich air crash. Reigning league champions United attracted an enthusiastic crowd of 35,872, but were overwhelmed by an inspired Rovers side who scored four times through Alfie Biggs (twice), Barrie Meyer and Geoff Bradford. Desmond Hackett in *The Daily Express* called Rovers the '£110 team with the million-dollar touch of class'.

# ONE SWALLOW

ENDING a run of five straight league defeats in the autumn of 2009, Rovers gave a first full league game to Ben Swallow against Carlisle United. Rovers scored two goals in the final eight minutes to register a 3-2 victory at the Memorial Stadium. Born in Cardiff in October 1989, Swallow had made his debut as a substitute in a cup game against Aldershot Town in August 2009 and appeared in four league matches from the bench, as well as in three separate cup competitions, prior to making his first senior start in the league.

## YOUNGEST OPPONENT

ALTHOUGH many players have appeared in league football aged 15 no opponent has faced Rovers in league action before their 16th birthday. The youngest of a plethora of 16-year-old opponents was the Notts County forward Bob Woolley, who played and scored against Rovers over Easter 1964.

1. Bob Woolley (Notts County) b. 29/12/47 .. pl. 09/04/64 ..16 years 102 days
2. Marvin Brown (Bristol City) ..b. 06/07/83 .. pl. 17/10/99 ..16 years 103 days
3. Lee Grant (York City) (sub)....b. 31/12/85 .. pl. 16/04/02 ..16 years 106 days
4. Jack Hobbs (Lincoln City) ......b. 18/08/88 .. pl. 15/01/05 ..16 years 150 days
5. David Worrall (Bury) ..............b. 12/06/90 .. pl. 18/11/06 ..16 years 159 days

## EASTVILLE ABLAZE

JUST a few hours after Rovers had opened their season with a draw at home to Orient in August 1980, the South Stand at Eastville burned down. The immediate aftermath of this fire was that the club's administrative offices and dressing rooms were destroyed and what was left of the stand, built in 1924, had to be pulled down. Rovers were forced to play their next three 'home' league games at Ashton Gate. In the long term, this incident helped precipitate Rovers' departure from the ground they had considered home since 1897 and meant a decade in footballing exile in Bath. Previously, back in April 1937, only the prompt actions of an alert watchman, Tom Berry, had prevented a storeroom fire from engulfing a whole stand at Eastville.

## THE GOAL THAT WON THE CHAMPIONSHIP

CENTRAL defender Brian Gayle spent the best part of two years with Rovers at the tail end of a long career. He was to represent Rovers in 23 league matches between 1996 and 1998. Earlier, in April 1992, Gayle had scored the goal that secured the league championship, but he would not have celebrated. For Gayle's own goal gave Leeds United a 3-2 victory over his own side, Sheffield United, of whom he was captain and thus presented their Yorkshire rivals with the points required to make them league champions.

AFTER THE SOUTH STAND FIRE, ROVERS PLAYED 'HOME' MATCHES AT ASHTON GATE

## EIGHT-GOAL TROJAN

WHEN he signed for Oldham Athletic in 1925 few could have imagined the impact Arthur Ormston would have. In his first game, he scored three times and followed up with five goals against Stoke City. Ormston's Rovers career was less extraordinary, though he was the club's top scorer in 1927/28. One contemporary reporter explained that "he works like a Trojan and simply revels in harassing full-backs and goalkeeper." Joining the Eastville club in June 1927, he scored 15 goals in 27 league appearances and also played league football for Chesterfield, Durham City, Coventry City, Barrow, Wigan Borough and Bradford City. Born in Northumberland in June 1900, the third son of William Ormston and Mary Dodderhill, he married Doreen Manders and died in Oldham, where he ran a pub, in October 1947, at a very early age. Doreen, 20 years his junior, died in January 2000, aged 79.

## ICED TEA

IN a bid to reward the brave few who had travelled on a freezing Tuesday night in February 1987 to Darlington to watch Rovers' Third Division fixture, Rovers' directors kindly organised for an urn of tea to provide their fans with much-needed half-time sustenance. Following a fairly poor and goalless first half, a plastic cup with tea was gratefully received. Seventeen-year-old Steve Yates made his debut, David Mehew scored as two goals in a mid-second-half minute left the score 1-1 and Rovers' cold fans discovered that, before the final whistle, the dregs in their cups had already frozen in the chilly north-eastern air.

## NIL-NIL AT HALF-TIME

THE most second-half goals scored in a league match featuring Rovers, following a goalless first half, is seven. This occurred in December 1974 when Rovers won 4-3 at Oldham Athletic's Boundary Park. There were six goals in the second half in March 1980 when Rovers drew 3-3 with Preston North End at Eastville and in January 1999, when Rovers defeated Reading 6-0 at the Madejski Stadium. When Rovers lost 7-0 at Warmley in September 1891, all seven goals were scored after half-time. On a national level, the most second-half goals following a goalless first half came when Exeter City defeated Aldershot 8-1 in a Third Division (South) fixture in May 1935.

## QUARTERED SHIRTS

ROVERS' distinctive quartered shirts have attracted a good deal of positive interest down the years. However, for many years, while other clubs performed in quarters, Rovers had worn a variety of kits. The blue-and-white quarters were adopted for the start of the 1931/32 season and were first worn for the 2-2 draw at Bournemouth in August 1931. Bert Young was the first Rovers player to score wearing the quarters. Between 1962 and 1973 these distinctive tops were discarded, but otherwise Rovers have worn quartered shirts ever since. Rovers wore red-and-white quarters for the 4-0 defeat at Cardiff City in November 1946. For the game in February 1955, Rovers wore blue-and-white quarters whilst Fulham were in red-and-white quarters. Both Bristol City, against Doncaster Rovers in the late 1950s, and Rochdale in 2005 have borrowed a set of Rovers' quartered kit after their own was mislaid in transit.

## MARY'S GRANDSON

ONE unsung hero of yesteryear was the full-back Frank Morley, who played in three games for Rovers prior to the club's elevation to the Southern League in 1899. Born in the spring of 1871 in Chipping Sodbury, Francis Thomas Morley was brought up with his father William at the home in Back Lane, Wickwar, Gloucestershire of his paternal grandparents Thomas and Mary Morley. An injury to the usually dependable Fred Lovett gave him the opportunity to appear in the side for the 1-0 victory away to Staple Hill in March 1896 and he then also played in two matches during the 1896/97 campaign. Frank Morley died in Chipping Sodbury in 1906, aged just 35.

## THE 'MIGHTY MIDGET'

ONLY 5ft 4ins. in height, Rovers' outside-left Bobby Gardiner scored ten goals in 66 league matches between 1937 and 1939. A Scotsman from Dundee, he formed half of a celebrated partnership at Dundee United with Arthur Milne (1915-97), the winner of one Scottish cap. During the 1935/36 season, these two diminutive forwards helped their side to 108 league goals, including 42 in the final six games, a feat unsurpassed in the Scottish league or the Football League. A baker by trade, Gardiner was to play in professional football in both France and Scotland after World War II and died in Dundee in April 1993.

## PENALTY SHOOT-OUTS

ROVERS have featured in 20 penalty shoot-outs, winning 14. Rovers' youth team beat Swindon Town 10-9 after 24 penalties in a shoot-out in November 1997.

| | | | |
|---|---|---|---|
| 09/05/1972 | Bristol City 1 Rovers 1 | Gloc Cup | Won 4-2 |
| 05/08/1972 | Rovers 0 Sheffield United 0 | Watney Cup | Won 7-6 |
| 10/08/1973 | Rovers 1 West Ham United 1 | Watney Cup | Won 6-5 |
| 01/05/1973 | Rovers 2 Bristol City 2 | Gloc Cup | Lost 3-5 |
| 12/08/1980 | Rovers 1 Exeter City 1 | League Cup | Won 7-6 |
| 06/02/1990 | Brentford 2 Rovers 2 | Leyland Daf | Won 4-3 |
| 14/03/1990 | Rovers 0 Walsall 0 | Leyland Daf | Won 3-2 |
| 05/08/1993 | Bristol City 1 Rovers 1 | Gloc Cup | Won 5-3 |
| 01/12/1993 | Rovers 2 Fulham 2 | Autoglass T | Lost 3-4 |
| 03/08/1994 | Rovers 0 Bristol City 0 | Gloc Cup | Won 11-10 |
| 10/01/1995 | Orient 0 Rovers 0 | Auto W | Lost 3-4 |
| 08/12/1998 | Walsall 2 Rovers 2 | Auto W | Lost 4-5 |
| 11/01/2000 | Northampton Town 0 Rovers 0 | Auto W | Won 5-3 |
| 27/09/2000 | Rovers 1 Everton 1 | League Cup | Won 4-2 |
| 31/01/2000 | Rovers 1 Yeovil Town 1 | LDV Vans | Won 5-4 |
| 22/08/2006 | Rovers 1 Luton Town 1 | League Cup | Lost 3-5 |
| 14/08/2007 | Rovers 1 Crystal Palace 1 | League Cup | Won 4-1 |
| 27/11/2007 | Rovers 3 Orient 3 | FA Cup | Won 6-5 |
| 22/01/2008 | Rovers 0 Fulham 0 | FA Cup | Won 5-3 |
| 01/09/2009 | Hereford United 0 Rovers 0 | League Cup | Lost 2-4 |

## THE MOST-CAPPED EUROPEAN

THE talented and creative midfielder Vitalijs Astafjevs, captain of Latvia, joined Rovers in 1999 and scored 16 goals in 110 league appearances. He joined Admira Wacker Mödling of Austria in July 2003 and later played for the Russian side Rubin Kazan and three Latvian sides. In March 2004, when he won his 100th international cap, he was presented with a bouquet of flowers prior to the game against Slovenia in Celje. He made his first appearance for Latvia in 1992, and captained the side against Honduras in November 2009 to set a new European international record of 158 caps, surpassing the previous record held by Estonia's Martin Reim.

## TAKING THE LEAD AGAINST ARSENAL

HAROLD 'Happy' Houghton was briefly the hero of Eastville. The mighty Arsenal came to town in January 1936 for an FA Cup tie; Rovers surely had no chance against a side that famously supplied seven of the England side that played Italy. However, after Cliff Bastin's penalty had been saved by Rovers' goalkeeper Jack Ellis, Houghton's low, long-range drive gave Rovers a sensational lead just three minutes before half-time. The Eastville faithful sensed a famous victory. Rovers' hopes of a shock win, though, were dashed; the game featured six goals and all were scored at the same end of the ground, as Arsenal, recovering after the break, won 5-1. Bastin and Ted Drake scored two apiece to break the hearts of the majority of the bumper crowd of 24,234 that raised a £3,552 profit for the club. Arsenal were to beat Sheffield Wednesday in that season's Wembley final.

## 'THE FLYING PIG FROM KIRKINTILLOCH'

JIM Eadie was the rock at the back for a very successful Rovers side in the early 1970s. Born in Alexandria, on the Banks of Loch Lomond in February 1947, Eadie's physical size and presence proved a daunting prospect for opposition forwards and he kept a clean sheet in 22 of the 46 games as Rovers, thanks in part to a 32-match unbeaten league run, secured promotion from Division Three in 1973/74. Formerly a plumber on the QE2, Eadie had experienced European football with Cardiff City before making 183 league appearances in goal for Rovers. He left in September 1977 to join Bath City.

## HOME MATCHES AT THE GATE

FOLLOWING the South Stand fire at Eastville in August 1980, Rovers were obliged to play three home league games at Ashton Gate. All three were drawn; 2-2 with Grimsby Town, and 0-0 with Oldham Athletic and Newcastle United. In addition, a League Cup tie against York City was won 1-0, thanks to an own goal from Steve Faulkner. To enable a large crowd to watch the derby game with Swindon Town in April 1987, Rovers switched their home game to Ashton Gate where, in front of a crowd of 8,196, Rovers led 3-1 before losing an eventful game 4-3.

## BLACK SATURDAY

THE Saturday immediately prior to Christmas has adopted the name Black Saturday, as attendances are notoriously down as a result of the conflicting demands of Christmas shopping. In certain years between the wars, FA Cup ties were played on this date, while other fixtures have succumbed to the inclement weather. To the end of the 2009/10 season, Rovers had won 27 league matches on Black Saturday, drawn 14 and lost 25; the largest win was 6-1 against Doncaster Rovers in 1956, and the heaviest defeat the same score against Millwall in 1927. The highest attendance was 31,995 at Notts County in 1949, beating the 27,863 at Leeds United in 2007. On the other hand, only 2,623 were at Rochdale in 2004, surpassing the previous lowest crowds of 3,240 at Blackpool in 1988 and 3,343 at Mansfield in 1938.

## ZED

WHEN Rovers fielded Bobby Zamora and Lee Zabek for the FA Cup tie against Preston North End in October 2000, they became the first league team to have two players in their side whose surnames began with the letter Z. The first opponent whose surname began with Z was Peter Zelem, who scored for Chester City against Rovers at Eastville in August 1981. Others have included Romeo Zondervan (Ipswich Town), Chris Zebroski (Wycombe Wanderers), Arjan de Zeeuw (Wigan Athletic), L'Andry Zahana-Oni (Luton Town), Gabriel Zakuani (Orient), Ruben Zadkovich (Notts County), Sofiane Zaaboub (Swindon Town) and Calvin Zola (Crewe Alexandra).

## LITHUANIA

A LITHUANIAN-born outside-right played for Luton Town against Rovers in each of the first four league meetings between the clubs. Louis Buckhalter was born in Zagaren, near the Latvian border, in 1890 and changed his name to Bookman on his arrival in Britain. He represented Bradford City and West Bromwich Albion, as well as appearing for Northern Ireland, and joined Luton Town in 1920. Rovers won all four matches in which Bookman was involved, including a 5-0 win at Eastville in March 1921. Bookman also represented Bedfordshire at cricket in 1921 and played cricket for Ireland between 1920 and 1929 as an opening left-handed batsman and slow left-arm bowler. He settled in Dublin, dying in June 1943.

## SEEING RED

AFTER Hereford United, Rovers attained a certain notoriety in having four men sent off in a league fixture. The game at Wigan Athletic in December 1997 was not viewed by most as dirty, but referee Kevin Lynch sent five men from the field. David Pritchard was dismissed for a second bookable offence on the stroke of half-time and, as the sides waited for the free kick to be taken, Jason Perry, Andy Tillson and Wigan's Graeme Jones were sent off for alleged fighting; Josh Low was sent off after 71 minutes for a second bookable offence. Rovers lost 3-0. Hereford United had received four red cards in their game against Northampton Town in September 1992 and there had also been five men dismissed in the Plymouth Argyle (three red cards) against Chesterfield (two red cards) fixture of February 1997.

## THE AUCHINLECK MINER

EVERY club has a one-game wonder and James Anderson Kedens was certainly one of those. Born in Auchinleck in April 1901, Jimmy Kedens was one of 13 children of Ayrshire miner William Kedens and his wife Helen Anderson. A miner by trade, he escaped this interminable drudgery in search of football. From Sherburn Rovers and Ardeer Thistle, he signed for Rovers in December 1926 and played the following month at Brighton where Rovers conceded two penalties for the second consecutive season and lost 7-0. He returned to Scotland the following May to work at the Glenburn pit and played for Glenburn Rovers until 1936. Unmarried and a lifelong pipe-smoker, he died in Prestwick in January 1975.

## MERE YOUTHS

THE five youngest players to have appeared for Rovers in Football League action, with the date of their first league match for the club, are:

1. Ronnie Dix ..... b. 05/09/12 ... pl. 25/02/28 ....... 15 years 173 days
2. Scott Sinclair .. b. 29/03/89 ... pl. 26/12/04 ....... 15 years 276 days
3. Simon Bryant . b. 22/11/82 ... pl. 28/08/99 ....... 16 years 279 days
4. Neil Slatter ..... b. 30/05/64 ... pl. 11/04/81 ....... 16 years 316 days
5. Steve Yates ...... b. 29/01/70 ... pl. 03/03/87 ......... 17 years 33 days

## ONLY TEN MEN

IN January 1893, Rovers started with only ten men against Trowbridge Town, as Frank Laurie arrived late; the game finished 2-2. At Clevedon in March 1890 and at Swindon Athletic three years later, Rovers had to borrow players to make up the numbers. Conversely, Rovers beat a ten-man Wells side 5-1 in March 1893, the following month Swindon Athletic started with only eight men and Rovers won 1-0, whilst Clifton played the entire game against Rovers in April 1897 with only nine men and Rovers, through a 'wretched performance' contrived to lose the game 2-0. Billy Beats, who scored 44 goals in 94 Southern League matches for Rovers, missed his train and failed to turn up for Port Vale's first Football League fixture; ten-man Vale lost 5-1 to Small Heath (now Birmingham City) in September 1892.

## MONTSERRAT

ELIZABETH Richards James, the mother of Albert John Cowlin, a Rovers player in late Victorian times, was born on the island of Montserrat; she married Nicholas Cowlin, a Somerset police constable. In recent years, there have been two further Rovers connections; a pair of Montserrat internationals have appeared for the opposition. Tefaye Bramble, born in July 1980, who scored against Antigua in his sole international match, played six times for Southend United against Rovers, scoring three goals, and a further four times for Stockport County. Junior Mendes, born in September 1976, scored once in two internationals for Montserrat and also played against Rovers in the league for Northampton Town, Mansfield Town and Notts County, as well as playing for Lincoln City against Rovers in the play-off semi-finals in 2007.

## PLASTIC

ROVERS played in four league fixtures on artificial pitches in matches played at Preston and Oldham, when these surfaces were a subject of Football League interest. The club's record was one win, one draw and two defeats. The sole win came at Preston in February 1990, when David Mehew scored the only goal of the game. Rovers also featured in an FA Cup tie on Luton Town's artificial pitch in January 1986. The game was lost 4-0 with the goals coming from former Bristol City striker Mick Harford, Ricky Hill, Marc North and a Tim Parkin own goal.

# THE RUSSIAN CENTRE-FORWARD

THE only player born in Russia to represent Rovers was not a star of the modern era, but Lewis Frank, whose sole appearance for Rovers came in a Bristol and District League game against Warmley in April 1891. With regular centre-forward Fred Yates unavailable, Frank stood in as Rovers, a goal behind at half-time, crashed 5-1 away to their local rivals, Archie Laurie scoring a late consolation goal. A Jewish immigrant from Russia, his family moved to Leeds when he was a child and it was there that he married in 1889 to Etty, a British national born in Germany. The couple settled in Bristol, where Lewis found work as a tailor. They had five children – David, Rebecca, Eli, Mary and Jacob – and lived in William Street in Bedminster.

# UGANDA

DURING the 1989/90 season, Rovers lost just five times in the league, a club record in the Football League years since 1920. One of these defeats took place on New Year's Day, a 3-1 loss at Rotherham United's Millmoor ground, where one of the three goals scored by the home side was credited to Bobby Williamson. Whilst no Rovers player has ever played football in Uganda, Williamson made a name for himself there. A Scotsman, the striker enjoyed a long career north of the border and also played in England, at West Bromwich Albion and Rotherham United; he managed several clubs either side of the border. He took over as national manager of Uganda in August 2008 and led The Cranes to victory in the December 2009 CECAFA Cup, defeating Rwanda 2-0 in the final in Nairobi.

# THE FABULOUS WILLIAMS BOYS

WHEN Rovers beat Wrexham 4-0 in a Third Division game at Eastville in December 1983, three players called Williams scored for the club. David Williams put Rovers ahead after a goalless first half and, after Ian Holloway had added a second, Geraint Williams and Brian Williams added further goals. It was the second occasion that three players with one surname had scored for a club in league football for, back in April 1927, three of the nine Keetley brothers, Tom, Frank and Harold, all scored as Doncaster Rovers defeated Durham City 5-1 in a Third Division (North) fixture.

# LONG-RANGE GOALS

PRIOR to Wycombe Wanderers' Second Division game against Rovers in December 1996, their manager Alan Smith said he would fine any player who shot from outside the penalty area. Despite this warning, Dave Carroll, Mickey Bell and Michael Simpson all scored with long-range shots against their manager's instructions. Rovers, who had never before lost a league game to Wycombe, surrendered a 3-1 lead and lost 4-3. Marcus Kelly gave non-league Rushden & Diamonds an 11th-minute FA Cup lead with a wind-assisted 40-yard shot at the Memorial Stadium in December 2007 – Rovers won 5-1. Orient's Sid Bishop scored with a 40-yard rocket in Rovers' 3-2 defeat at Brisbane Road in February 1961. Perhaps the longest-range goal scored by any Rovers player in a league fixture was the shot from the halfway line with which Vaughan Jones scored in the 3-2 win at home to Notts County at Twerton Park in September 1989. Ellis Compton scored from 40 yards during the first half of Rovers' 8-0 wartime win at home to RAVC in April 1919; he added a second-half penalty for good measure. The future Rovers defender David Lee scored with a 50-yard free kick from inside his own half of the field while playing for Chelsea reserves against Rovers reserves in the Avon Combination League in the late 1980s.

# MOST LEAGUE APPEARANCES

A GIANT of a central defender, Stuart Taylor joined Rovers in August 1965 and made his league debut the following April against Workington. This proved to be the first of 546 league appearances, a club record that brought him 28 goals, prior to joining Bath City as player-manager in May 1980.

| | |
|---|---|
| Stuart Taylor | 546 |
| Harry Bamford | 486 |
| Jack Pitt | 467 |
| Geoff Bradford | 461 |
| Harold Jarman | 452 |
| George Petherbridge | 452 |
| Ray Warren | 450 |
| Alfie Biggs | 424 |
| Bobby Jones | 420 |

## THREE GOALS IN A SEASON

WHEN Rovers won 5-3 at Oldham Athletic in May 1968, the Latics' Ian Wood scored all three of their goals in the defeat. These were the only goals that Wood scored all season. The same occurred in May 1925 when Rovers lost 4-1 at Reading, for whom Herbert Davey scored his only three goals of the season to register a hat-trick. Similarly, Frank Gill scored just four times in the league for Tranmere Rovers during the 1969/70 season, but three of these came when Rovers were defeated 5-2 at Prenton Park in April 1970. Notts County's Ron Wylie scored five league goals in 1955/56, three of them in their 5-2 victory over Rovers in December 1955. Frank Richardson's three goals as Plymouth Argyle won 3-1 at Eastville in August 1921 were scored on his league debut.

## BLOOD AND GUTS

ONE of the most unlikely of draws was the product of a tempestuous home local derby with Yeovil Town in October 2004. After dominating early play, Rovers had fallen behind to a deflected Paul Terry goal. In first-half injury-time, the visitors' Gavin Williams crashed to the floor and Rovers' midfielder Dave Savage, who had clearly lashed out, though without making contact, was sent off by referee Phil Crossley. Within a minute, defender Steve Elliott became the second Rovers player to be dismissed as the atmosphere turned sour. Swiftly 2-0 down, nine-man Rovers then staged a comeback of epic proportions, as first James Hunt and then, with four minutes remaining, man-of-the-match Junior Agogo completed Rovers' unexpected yet, on the basis of their second-half display, well-merited recovery.

## FREE KICK PIONEER

A NEW rule for the start of the 1903/04 season was that certain free kicks were now direct. The first player to score from a direct free kick in the Football League was Arthur Rowley, who opened the scoring as Port Vale lost 3-2 to Bolton Wanderers at Vale Park in Division Two in September 1903. Born in Stoke-upon-Trent in 1870, Rowley had previously been with Rovers for the 1899/1900 season, in which he appeared in two Southern League matches as a left-back. He played in a 3-0 defeat at Reading and a 1-0 home defeat against New Brompton.

## JOHN RUMENS

EVERY club's history is littered with one-game wonders. John Rumens, a 19-year-old centre-half, played in the 2-0 defeat at St. George in September 1891. Rumens was the son of a brewer's salesman from Lamberhurst, Kent, Thomas Rumens, who met Harriet Adams through work when she was employed at the Black Lion in Oxford. The pair married in Bethnal Green in the autumn of 1863 and had three daughters before John was born in the autumn of 1871. The family moved to Bristol, where Thomas was to die in 1897 at the age of 64. John was a bootmaker's clicker living in St. Philip and St. Jacob's but, after his brief spell with Rovers, he moved to Eve Road in Easton, from where he married Sarah Biddlecombe in the spring of 1908.

## HAT-TRICK!

THE oldest Rovers player to record a league hat-trick was Bill Culley. The veteran striker was 34 years and 232 days old when his three goals helped defeat Swindon Town on April 15th 1927. Sixty-one years later to the day, David Mehew became the youngest hat-trick scorer for Rovers, his three goals helping Rovers to a 4-0 victory at York City's Bootham Crescent in April 1988; he was 20 years and 168 days, nine days younger than Nathan Ellington when he scored three times against Leyton Orient on Boxing Day 2001. On the other hand, the veteran former Manchester United centre-forward Stan Pearson scored three of Bury's seven goals against Rovers on Christmas Day 1956 to become – at 37 years and 349 days – the oldest man to record a league hat-trick against Rovers. A year later, on December 28th 1957, West Ham United's John Smith, just 18 years and 358 days old, became the youngest to do so.

## DISABILITIES

HUGH Adcock, a former England international who scored once in thirteen league games for Rovers in the 1935/36 season, sadly went blind later in life. An outside-right who had spent many years with Leicester City, he died in Coalville, Leicestershire in October 1975 at the age of 72. Bert Densley, who played in 23 league games in goal for Rovers during the 1920s, had both his legs amputated late in life. He died in Bristol in the spring of 1982, aged 78.

## MATCH ABANDONED

26/11/21 ..Reading 1 Rovers 3 ................................. abandoned, 52 mins, fog

07/12/29 ..Rovers 0 Bournemouth 1 .........abandoned, 45 mins, waterlogged

17/02/51 ..Rovers 2 Norwich City 1..........abandoned, 60 mins, waterlogged

26/12/62 ..Reading 1 Rovers 0 ............................... abandoned, 60 mins, frost

09/03/82 ..Rovers 1 Oxford United 1........abandoned, 64 mins, waterlogged

30/11/85 ..Chesterfield 1 Rovers 1........................... abandoned, 45 mins, fog

15/12/01 ..Rovers 0 Hartlepool United 0.............. abandoned, 12 mins, frost

## SCANDAL!

ROVERS hit the national headlines for all the wrong reasons in April 1963 following a bribery scandal involving the oddly named goalkeeper Esmond Million and the club's top scorer Keith Williams. Though others were also implicated, both players admitted attempting to fix the result of the relegation clash with Bradford Park Avenue. Million had stood to earn £300 if Rovers lost but, ironically, the match was drawn 2-2. Both players were fined £50 in court and banned for life by the Football Association. Million, who had played 38 times for Rovers in the league, returned to his native north-east and became a bus driver in Middlesbrough. Williams, who had scored 18 goals in his 49 league games with Rovers, emigrated to South Africa.

## AGGERS' CRICKET COACH

THE famous England bowler and subsequent BBC cricket commentator Jonathan Agnew was coached in cricket by a former Rovers player. Les Berry was cricket coach at Uppingham School from 1952 to 1980 and 'Aggers' was just one of a multitude of young enthusiastic cricketers who passed through the safe hands of the former goalkeeper. Born in Dorking in April 1906, Berry played four times for Rovers in the 1930/31 league season, but was better known as Leicestershire captain. A right-handed batsman, he scored over 30,000 runs in county cricket, including a score of 232 against Sussex at Leicester in 1930. He died in Leicestershire in February 1985.

# ENGLAND AWAITS

HAVING played for Rovers in their 1-0 win at Wrexham in 1979, central defender Mike England had to wait over six years for his second appearance for the side. In the meantime, he had left and rejoined the club, re-appearing for the second of his 18 league matches when Rovers again enjoyed a single-goal victory in Wales, defeating Swansea City 1-0 in September 1985. Rhys Evans played in goal for Rovers against Bury in March 2000 on loan and next appeared for Rovers in September 2009 against Wycombe Wanderers, after a gap of nine years and six months. Even including those whose careers were interrupted by war, Evans' gap between appearances for Rovers is the longest in the club's history. Similarly, Tony Gough made one league appearance for Rovers in April 1959; the second league game of his career was for Swindon Town in 1970. He played league football in the 1950s and 1970s, but not in the 1960s.

# FUTURE PIRATES SCORING

THREE Rovers players had already scored for the club before they signed for Rovers, and two never managed it after signing. Kevin Moore scored an own goal in August 1980, when playing for Grimsby Town against Rovers in Division Two; he joined Rovers on loan in 1992, scoring once in eleven league appearances. Keith Viney scored an own goal at Eastville in December 1982 in Exeter City's 4-4 draw in Division Three and signed for Rovers on loan in 1988 – he played in two league matches. Scott Shearer scored an own goal in April 2004 whilst playing for Rushden & Diamonds and joined Rovers in 2005, appearing in goal in 47 league matches.

# THE OLDEST MAN

WHEN Neil McBain played for New Brighton as an emergency goalkeeper against Hartlepool United in March 1947, he became, at 51 years of age, the oldest player to appear in the Football League. McBain, a Scottish international wing-half, had scored one of the goals through which Watford won 4-3 against Rovers in February 1930. Born in November 1895, McBain also played for Liverpool, Everton and Manchester United, before becoming the only man born in the 19th century to play in post-war league football. He died in 1974.

# BOWLS

JACK Bethune, who played 30 times at full-back for Rovers in 1920/21, represented England at indoor bowls in the 1936 and 1938 series. Fred Leamon, a Channel Islander who was Rovers' top scorer in 1946/47, represented Wales over 20 times at bowls. Bob Plenderleith, having played 22 times for Rovers in 1929/30 as a centre-half, later worked in Sunderland where he was the town's bowls champion. Billy Baldwin, the scorer of three goals in four league games for Gillingham against Rovers between 1934 and 1936, was an accomplished bowls player and won the All-England Bowls Cup in 1965. Jimmy Carr, a member of the England bowls team at the 1954 Empire Games in Vancouver, played for Watford against Rovers in 1914, and in six Football League matches for Reading against Rovers, scoring at Eastville in December 1920.

# "MISTER ENGLISH"

WILLY Garbutt, who played for Arsenal in their 1-0 FA Cup win against Rovers in February 1907, was coach at Genoa from 1914 – and again from 1946 – Roma from 1927, Napoli two years later and Athletic Bilbao from 1935. Whilst at Genoa, 'Mister English' became the first professional football manager in Italy where he was a charismatic tactical visionary and legendary pipe smoker. Under his guidance, Genoa won three consecutive Italian titles, the most recent coming in 1924. Another Englishman who moved to Italy was Les Lievesley who played seven times for Torquay United against Rovers (1933-37) and in both of Crystal Palace's league fixtures against Rovers in the 1937/38 season. He was one of the 31 fatalities in the Superga crash in Italy in May 1949 that wiped out the Torino team – Lievesley was coach.

# MISSING REFEREE

IN May 1923, referee H. C. Curtis failed to arrive for Rovers' league match at Swansea. Linesman U. Jones of Ton Pentre took the whistle and D. Sambrooke of Swansea ran the line as Rovers won 1-0. Tosh Parker scored the only goal of the game direct from a corner. In December 1935, referee B. Ames arrived late for Rovers' league game at Exeter and a home player took over temporarily as linesman. Mr Ames arrived 20 minutes into the game and took over his duties at that point for a match that Rovers lost 3-1.

## DOCTOR IN THE HOUSE

HAVE you heard of the Rovers hat-trick scorer who became a doctor? In September 1888, Rovers defeated Kingswood 8-0 away from home and Harry Cade scored three of the side's goals. Born in Bristol in March 1863, Henry Lowless Cade was the middle of three children and only son to Henry Cade (1829-1899), and his wife Eliza (1828-1878). He trained in London as a General Practitioner and was sent on placement in the Bristol area, during which time he played 13 times for Rovers as a centre-forward, notching seven goals. Graduating from St. Thomas' Hospital in 1892, he worked for many years as a General Practitioner in Wallington, Surrey. He died in Camberwell at the tail end of 1925, aged 62.

## SINGAPORE

DANIEL Bennett, who played in Wrexham's 3-0 win against Rovers in November 2002, played 47 times for Singapore. Born in Great Yarmouth, he moved to Singapore and changed nationality. Terry Butcher, who opposed Rovers in the FA Cup with Ipswich Town in January 1985, was born in Singapore. Kim Grant, a Ghanaian who played league football against Rovers with Luton Town, Millwall and Charlton Athletic, played for Geylang United in Singapore in 2006/07.

## NIL-NIL

THERE was little goal action at Eastville in the early 1920s. Rovers played out a club seasonal record of ten goalless draws in the 1922/23 season including three in succession over New Year. However, between goalless draws with Barnsley in March 1959 and Walsall in December 1961, Rovers played a club record 114 league matches in which at least one goal was scored.

## TRANSYLVANIA

FEW connections exist between Rovers and Romania. Mark Burke, though – who joined Rapid Bucharest in the summer of 2001 – scored twice when Wolves defeated Rovers 5-1 at Molineux in November 1992. Alex Nyarko, a Ghanaian who played for Everton in their League Cup clashes with Rovers in September 2000, spent the 1994/95 season with Steaua Bucharest.

## FIRST-HALF HAT-TRICKS

ON 14 ocassions, a Rovers player has recorded a hat-trick before half-time in a league fixture. Vic Lambden and Peter Beadle have achieved this feat on two separate occasions each. In the case of Sid Leigh, Lambden against Aldershot and Lambert, the player concerned went on to register a fourth goal after the interval. No Rovers player has ever scored five times in a league encounter. Gould's three goals were scored on his debut for the club and represent the only hat-trick he scored in a Rovers shirt. When Bannister scored his goals at Brighton, Alan Warboys weighed in with four of his own. In every case when a Rovers player has scored a first-half hat-trick, the match was won. By means of contrast, the former Rovers striker Gareth Taylor, playing for Burnley at home to Watford in April 2003, had scored three times before the interval only for his side, 5-4 down at the break, to lose 7-4.

| | | | |
|---|---|---|---|
| Sid Leigh | 02/05/1921 | D3S | Rovers 5 Exeter City 0 |
| Ernie Whatmore | 30/04/1927 | D3S | Rovers 4 Palace 1 |
| Albert Taylor | 16/03/1935 | D3S | Rovers 5 Newport County 3 |
| Frank Curran | 25/03/1939 | D3S | Rovers 5 Swindon Town 0 |
| Vic Lambden | 29/03/1948 | D3S | Rovers 7 Aldershot 1 |
| Vic Lambden | 14/04/1952 | D3S | Rovers 6 Colchester United 0 |
| Geoff Bradford | 04/09/1954 | D2 | Rovers 4 Derby County 1 |
| Peter Hooper | 26/12/1956 | D2 | Rovers 6 Bury 1 |
| Brian Godfrey | 04/09/1971 | D3 | Rovers 7 Bradford City 1 |
| Bruce Bannister | 01/12/1973 | D3 | Brighton 2 Rovers 8 |
| Bobby Gould | 15/10/1977 | D2 | Rovers 4 Blackburn Rovers 1 |
| Peter Beadle | 30/11/1996 | D2 | Rovers 4 Bury 3 |
| Peter Beadle | 28/12/1997 | D2 | Rovers 5 AFC Bournemouth 3 |
| Rickie Lambert | 25/10/2008 | L1 | Rovers 4 Southend United 2 |

## THE TEAM THAT EARNED MONEY

SHREWSBURY Town's team that lost 2-0 to Rovers in February 1997 had earned the Blues more money in transfer fees than the team had actually cost. Mickey Brown's two earlier transfers had generated a £120,000 profit, whilst only Mark Dempsey, Darren Currie, Dave Walton (£25,000 each) and Ian Stevens (£20,000) had required transfer fees. Marcus Browning and Peter Beadle scored Rovers' goals before a crowd of 4,924.

## CAUGHT ON THE REBOUND

THERE was an era when Rovers supporters could count on the wholesale effort and thunderbolt shot of outside-left Peter Hooper. His tally of 101 league goals for Rovers leaves him in joint fifth place in the club's all-time goalscorers list. The unstoppable power in his shots has gone down in club folklore. One astonishing story that is often told features the penalty awarded late on in the home Second Division fixture with Leicester City in September 1957, with the score standing at 1-1. Hooper hit the spot kick with such force that, on striking the base of the post, the ball rebounded past the waiting players and down the pitch, where Leicester's Tommy McDonald was able to break away and score what proved to be the winning goal.

## BIZARRE INJURIES

NUMEROUS careers have been curtailed by serious injuries, while others have been merely affected by unusual accidents. Jack Smith, who had trained as a dentist before playing in four league games as a full-back for Rovers in the 1934/35 season, found his career had prematurely ended after a bus ran over his foot during a wartime black-out. When Rovers reserves beat Watford reserves 2-0 at Eastville in April 1922, two opponents, James Short and Frank Pankhurst, broke their collar-bones in separate incidents. The former Rovers striker Lee Thorpe broke his arm in three places while arm-wrestling team mate René Howe on the team bus en route to Rochdale's play-off game at Darlington in May 2008.

## HOLLAND 2 ROVERS 3

CROSSING the English Channel overnight after a Saturday fixture, Rovers took on and beat the Dutch national side in November 1930 in Amsterdam. Rovers won 3-2, with Ronnie Dix scoring twice and Arthur Attwood once. Gerrit Hulsman scored both the Dutch goals. Contemporary reporters expressed surprise that a third-tier English side had only won so narrowly against Holland. Rovers were to tour the Netherlands again in 1932 and 1948, as well as playing in France in 1933. In May 1933, Rovers were to lose 3-1 to AC Milan in a match played in Nice, with George McNestry scoring from the spot. McNestry was to score again four days later when Rovers lost 3-1 to a French XI.

# LIFE BEGINS...

OF a total of 19 players, 15 of whom were outfield players, who have opposed Rovers in league action after their 40th birthday, the oldest was the Bristol City goalkeeper Alex Ferguson, who was 43 years old when he appeared in the first post-war derby in September 1946. The most recent 40-year-old opponent was Andy Hessenthaler, who made his final league appearance against Rovers in November 2006. On a national level, ten different players have appeared in league football after their 44th birthday. The oldest former Rovers player to play against the club was John Taylor, who played for Colchester United in October 2003 six days short of his 39th birthday.

Alex Ferguson (Bristol City) ........ b. 05/08/03 ...pl. 28/09/46   43 yrs 55 days
Jack Page (Merthyr T) .................. b. 24/03/86 ...pl. 16/03/29 42 yrs 358 days
Mick Burns (Ipswich T) ............... b. 07/06/08 ...pl. 31/03/51 42 yrs 239 days
Tommy Hutchison (Swan City) . b. 22/09/47 ...pl. 24/02/90 42 yrs 156 days
Peter Shilton (Derby County) ..... b. 18/09/49 ...pl. 15/02/92 42 yrs 151 days

# MOTHER BORN IN THE RAJ

CLARENCE Leslie Hughes was the son of Henry and Ena Hughes of Middlesex, though his mother had been born in India in 1863. He was the second of four children, born in Brentford, Middlesex on January 2nd 1896 and moved to Bristol at an early age. Inside-forward Hughes enjoyed two spells with Bristol City, sandwiching between them the 1919/20 season at Eastville, in which he scored twice in five Southern League matches for Rovers. He married a Bristol girl and settled in Weston-super-Mare, where he died in May 1989, aged 93. Two Indian-born players, Hubert Ashton and Charles Preedy, have played league football for Rovers. Indian international Baichung Bhatia played for Bury against Rovers in October 2000 and other Indian-born opponents include Ricky Heppolette (Orient), Dave Chadwick (Southampton, Halifax Town and AFC Bournemouth), Eric Lancelotte (Brighton & Hove Albion) and the Swindon Town pair of Mark Payne and Cornelius Hogan. When Rovers lost a Western League game 10-0 to Spurs in September 1907, eight of the goals were scored by Jimmy Pass, who was born in Juffulpore in November 1883.

## MINUTES WITHOUT CONCEDING

THE longest Football League run without conceding a goal in Rovers' history is 707 minutes. This was achieved by goalkeeper Jim Eadie, who was between the sticks for the 1-1 draw at home to Hereford United in September 1973 and then kept six consecutive clean sheets before letting in a goal in the 1-1 draw at home to Port Vale the following month. Nigel Martyn also kept six consecutive clean sheets on two occasions in the league, the longer length of time being 645 minutes in the autumn of 1989, following a 1-0 defeat at Bolton Wanderers, a run that ended with a 1-1 draw at Cardiff City. He also kept six consecutive clean sheets between the 3-1 defeat at Preston in April 1988 and a 2-1 loss at Brighton & Hove Albion a month later.

## FOUR HOME GROUNDS

ONE extraordinary record held by Gary Penrice is that he scored league goals for Rovers in home matches on four different grounds. His first goal at Eastville came against York City in May 1985, he scored in Rovers' fixture against Swindon Town at Ashton Gate in April 1987, he added goals in four consecutive seasons at Twerton Park and his first goal at the Memorial Stadium was Rovers' first of three against Carlisle United in August 1997. Phil Purnell and Ian Holloway both scored goals on three different home grounds in the league for Rovers. Bob Horsey represented Rovers in competitive football on five different home grounds between 1883 and 1899, namely Purdown, Three Acres, Durdham Downs, Rudgeway and Eastville.

## EUROPEAN HAT-TRICK

TWO Rovers players have scored a hat-trick in European club football. Alan Ball scored three times as Everton defeated the Icelandic side Keflavik 6-2 in a European Cup first-round tie in September 1970, en route to a 9-2 aggregate victory. Ball joined Rovers in January 1983 and scored twice in 17 league matches. Sandy Allan completed a hat-trick of headers as Cardiff City beat Mjoendalen of Norway 5-1 in a European Cup Winners' Cup first-round game in October 1969. The Welsh side won 12-2 on aggregate. Allan scored 18 goals in 51 (plus seven as substitute) league matches after joining Rovers from the Ninian Park side later that season.

## FEELING SHEEPISH

DID you hear the story about the player with a league championship medal who had a goal disallowed because some sheep had strayed on to the pitch? Well, having already scored for Taunton United against Torquay United in an FA Cup tie in October 1925, the former Rovers outside-right Joe Walter found a second effort disallowed as two sheep had entered the field of play before he shot. Walter played for Rovers in 82 league games, scoring 12 goals, and won a league championship medal with Huddersfield Town in 1923/24, as well as making a handful of appearances the following campaign as the Yorkshire club retained the league title. A guest at the opening of the McAlpine Stadium in Huddersfield in August 1994, Walter died in Bristol in May 1995, at the age of 99.

## REVERBERATING CRACK

FOR the opening game of the 1921/22 season against Plymouth Argyle, Rovers featured a debutant left-back in Jack Stockley. During the course of the match, Stockley's leg was broken in a tackle and the crack from the bone was heard all around the ground. The game was held up for a considerable time and Stockley was out of action for eight months. In an incident oddly reminiscent of the earlier one, Rovers' debutant left-back Graeme Power dislocated his shoulder during Rovers' home game against Plymouth Argyle in August 1997. Other players were not so lucky; Rovers' Tommy Cook, Dick Sheppard, Bernard Hall, Andrew Evans, Frank Allcock and Kenny Hibbitt all found their careers ended by broken bones suffered on the pitch playing for Rovers.

## DEBUT PENALTY SAVES

RYAN Clarke developed an uncanny knack, early in his career, of saving penalty kicks on his debut. First, he saved a penalty at Rochdale in April 2002 on his full Rovers debut, though the kick was later retaken successfully. In October 2004, he went on loan to Southend United and saved a spot kick in his first game at home to Shrewsbury Town. The following month, he was loaned to Kidderminster Harriers, for whom he saved a penalty at Port Vale on his debut. By December 2004, Clarke had played for three clubs in only ten matches, but incredibly under a total of eleven managers.

## ALFIE BIGGS

WHEN the Busby Babes came to Eastville in January 1956, Alfie Biggs scored twice as Rovers recorded a famous 4-0 victory to send Manchester United out of the FA Cup. Born in Bristol in February 1936, Biggs was to score 178 goals in his 424 league matches for Rovers, only his team mate Geoff Bradford having scored more frequently for the side. 'The Baron', as he became known on account of his dress sense, scored four hat-tricks for the club and was Rovers' Player of the Year in 1966/67. The 30 league goals he scored in 1963/64 has not been surpassed since, Rickie Lambert falling one short in 2008/09. Biggs, an Eastville folk hero, also enjoyed brief spells with Preston North End, Walsall and Swansea City and now lives in Poole.

## STRETCHED-OUT GOALS

WHEN the veteran midfielder Terry Paine scored for Hereford United against Rovers at Edgar Street over Easter 1977, it was more than 16 years since he had first scored in the league against the Eastville club. This eclipsed a record previously held by former Rovers youngster Gilbert Alsop, who scored against the club either side of World War II.

16 years 22 days ....... Terry Paine ............... 20/03/61 BR 4 So'ton 2
.......................................................... 11/04/77 Hereford U. 1 BR 1
15 years 270 days ..... Gilbert Alsop ..31/03/31 Coventry C. 5 BR 1
.................................................................. 26/12/46 Walsall 2 BR 0

## THE FIRST IRISH CONNECTION

IT is likely that the first player born on the Emerald Isle who represented Rovers in action was Alexander Gallagher. An inside-left, he played in just one game for the side, when Trowbridge Town defeated Rovers 5-2 in Wiltshire in January 1892, Bill Rogers scoring both Rovers' goals. Twenty-nine years old at the time, Gallagher was born in Armagh, now Northern Ireland, in 1862 and moved over to Bristol to work in the horse trade. His sister Mary and her husband Hugh McKeran owned a house in Sherbourne Road, St. George and Alexander based himself there, working locally as a stable groom. Nine Rovers players have represented Northern Ireland in international football, whilst six have played for Eire.

## KEITH VALLE

DURING Rovers' exile in Bath between 1986 and 1996, one notable character at matches at Twerton Park was the announcer Keith Valle. Noted for his humour, his timing and his propensity to mispronounce players' names, Keith famously told West Brom supporters in May 1991 that the final-day point they had gained was enough to avoid relegation; it was not. When Manchester City brought on Gary Flitcroft as a substitute in a League Cup tie at Twerton Park in October 1992, his name was given as "Gary Flipflop". On another occasion, the referee was announced as "wearing a pink crash helmet"; a bald-headed referee then ran on to the pitch. Keith Valle left the job in 1994 after inappropriate comments about the name of Bristol City's Junior Bent had caused controversy.

## FIRST LEAGUE MATCH

CHANGES to the structure of the Football League in the summer of 1920 meant that the Southern League en masse became Division Three and Rovers, along with many familiar names, found themselves facing the same clubs as before but in a different guise. Rovers' first league game was at Millwall in August 1920 and a crowd of 25,000 saw the home side score twice after half-time to secure victory. The opening goal came after 52 minutes when 'Banger' Voisey shot home from the edge of the area and, seven minutes later, Rovers' defeat was sealed when goalkeeper Harry Stansfield lost the flight of the ball in the sun and Jimmy Broad headed home the second.

## FRED FOOT'S SAGA

IN October 1882, a year before Rovers' formation, there was a fatality in the great floods along the River Frome. Frederick Charles Foot, a baker's delivery man, aged 19, was bringing bread from Williams bakery in Lower Easton to waiting customers when he and his pony were swept away by floodwater along Mina Road by the railway bridge. Despite concerted efforts from three locals and a policeman, both Fred Foot and his pony drowned. This was the only recorded drowning in several years' flooding during this era. It would appear that Foot had migrated to the city in search of employment for, though several viable possibilities exist nationally, there is no locally-recorded birth that matches his details.

## AMERICAN FOOTBALL

THE only footballer to have played league football against Rovers, and also appeared in an American Football side, was Bobby Howfield. Born inWatford in December 1936, he played league football for Watford, Crewe Alexandra, Aldershot and Fulham, notably scoring three goals in Fulham's 10-1 win against Ipswich Town on Boxing Day 1963 He played once against Rovers, when Watford lost at home 1-0 to a Keith Williams goal in December 1962. Howfield spent many years in gridiron football with Denver Broncos (1968-70) and New York Jets (1971-74), kicking 76 field goals from 119 attempts and adding 127 extra points from 134 attempts. More recently, his son Ian Howfield played for the Houston Oilers in 1991.

## GOLDEN GOAL

PRIOR to the 1995/96 season, a number of competitions introduced the 'golden goal' whereby, if a match was level after 90 minutes, play continued into extra time on a first-goal-wins basis. Most famously, Germany defeated the Czech Republic 2-1 in the 1996 European Championship Final at Wembley, thanks to Oliver Bierhoff's 95th-minute golden goal. Rovers won an Auto Windscreens Shield game 2-1 at Fulham in January 1996 when Marcus Stewart scored his second goal of the game in extra time, the only golden goal Rovers have ever scored. Conversely, the only one the club conceded was in the same competition at Walsall two years later, when Frenchman Roger Boli scored just 45 seconds into extra time.

## HOME DEBUT AWAY FROM HOME

FOR the 1996/97 season, Rovers were scheduled to play home games at the Memorial Stadium, but in fact played the opening fixture at Twerton Park, Bath. For this reason, both Matt Lockwood and Lee Martin made their club debuts in a home match played in a different city. Aiden McCaffrey and Bob Lee also made their home debuts for Rovers in fixtures played at Ashton Gate, following the Eastville fire of August 1980. Paul Bradshaw's first 'home' game for Rovers was the fixture against Swindon Town over Easter 1987 played at Bristol City's Ashton Gate; ironically his next appearance was against Bristol City in the goalless draw at Twerton Park eight days later.

## FIVE IN FIVE

ONLY one Rovers player has managed to score a goal in each of his first five league outings for the club. Syd Holcroft was an inside-forward who was born in Aston, Birmingham in August 1901 and joined Rovers in May 1924 after a career with Hednesford Town and Stourbridge. His goalscoring career was an unorthodox one, though, for his five early goals in 1924/25 proved to be the only ones he registered that season. It took more than a year for him to score again but when he did, he notched a hat-trick against Queens Park Rangers. Holcroft was transferred to Willenhall in 1927, having scored nine goals in his 33 league appearances in a Rovers shirt. He died in May 1934 in Birmingham, aged only 32.

## WATNEY CUP

ROVERS qualified for the 1972 Watney Cup because of their goalscoring record the previous season. The top-scoring sides in each division, except for those who had been promoted or qualified for European tournaments, met in a knock out competition. Rovers defeated Wolves 2-0 at Eastville and Burnley 2-0 at Turf Moor, Bruce Bannister scoring in both games, to qualify for the August 1972 final. Ironically, for a tournament designed to reward high goalscoring, the Eastville final was goalless. After 13 consecutive penalties had been scored, Rovers' goalkeeper Dick Sheppard saved Ted Hemsley's spot kick to give Rovers victory before a crowd of 19,768. Tom McAlister, United's goalkeeper in the final, was to play for Rovers on loan in February 1981.

## THE FOOTBALLING WIZARD OF WOOKEY HOLE

ONE former Rovers player was born at Wookey Hole in Somerset. The son of Joseph McEwan – a paper-maker from Denbighshire and his wife Harriet from Kent – James Scarson McEwan was born in the village in the spring of 1871. His parents had moved there because of the paper industry and James followed his father's profession. He was on Rovers' books between 1896 and 1898, playing in five games for the first team as an outside-right and scoring once against Staple Hill in October 1896. Around that time, he married Ellen and the 1901 census records him as resident in Wookey Hole with his wife and their three children, William, Edith and Catherine.

## MEMORIAL STADIUM

AFTER an absence of ten years, Rovers made their eagerly awaited return to Bristol in 1996. The professionalism of rugby union, and progressive links between rugby and football clubs, led Rovers to a groundshare scheme with Bristol Rugby Club. "We're back in Bristol at last," said Gordon Pearce on Rovers' return, "on the right side of town. It's the best thing since sliced bread." Rovers' first game on the ground was the 1-1 draw with Stockport County in August 1996, with Lee Archer scoring the first goal on the pitch. When the rugby club experienced financial difficulties, the Memorial Stadium Company bought the ground in 1998 for £2.3 million and Rovers became sole tenants. It remained "homely, friendly and a little bit ramshackle" (John Inverdale, October 2007). Bristol Rugby Club had moved to the ground in September 1921 in an opening ceremony performed by G. B. Britton, the Lord Mayor of Bristol. The six-and-a-half acres, formerly part of Buffalo Bill's Field, had been used as wartime allotments but were released in 1920 by the Ministry of Agriculture. The ground was dedicated to the memory of 300 local rugby players who had been killed in World War I and the first game there was Bristol's 19-3 win against Cardiff in September 1921. In October 1996, both Rovers and Bristol Rugby Club played home fixtures on the same day, Rovers playing out a goalless draw with Blackpool in the afternoon before Bristol lost 18-16 to the French side Narbonne in an evening fixture. By the summer of 2010, Rovers had played 321 league matches on the ground against 72 different sides, winning 136 and losing 92. The most frequent score, on 40 occasions, was 1-1. There had been eighteen red cards for Rovers players and 51 for opponents. Stuart Campbell's 120 league appearances on the ground are more than any other player, his 100th league match at The Mem being against Millwall in September 2009, Steve Elliott (106) and Craig Disley (101 – 99 times for Rovers) also played in one hundred league games there. Jamie Cureton (33), had scored the most league goals for Rovers on the ground, ahead of Rickie Lambert (31 – 29 of these for Rovers) and Richard Walker (30). The youngest player to appear in league football on the pitch was Scott Sinclair on Boxing Day 2004 at the age of 15 years and 275 days, whilst the oldest was Barnet's Andy Hessenthaler, aged 41 years 101 days in November 2006. Wycombe Wanderers had played in nine league matches there, more than any club, whilst the highest attendance was the 12,011 for the FA Cup quarter-final against West Bromwich Albion in March 2008.

## THE LION TAMER

FOLLOWING an incident whilst at Southampton when he had entered a lion's cage at a travelling circus in town, George Seeley was known thereafter as 'The Lion Tamer'. Born in Ventnor on the Isle of Wight, George Alfred Seeley joined Southampton in 1896 from Gordon Avenue and, after a stint with Bristol St. George, signed for Rovers later that calendar year. During his time with Rovers, Seeley played in 14 games and scored three times, all three goals coming in a single match against West Bromwich Albion reserves in November 1897, a game that was lost. An inside-left, he was to return to Southampton in 1898, later playing for New Brompton, Queens Park Rangers and Orient before leaving Southern League football in 1905. He died in Ventnor in October 1921.

## ROVERS 3 CHELSEA 0

THE very late 1970s saw Chelsea's fortunes wane and the club that had won the league in 1955 and FA Cup in 1970 spent several seasons in Division Two, where they were defeated by Rovers on three occasions. In February 1980, a strong Chelsea side came to Eastville and suffered a three-goal defeat. Striker Shaun Penny scored twice, and midfielder Tony Pulis once, before a crowd of 14,176. There was trouble at this game, as a small section of visiting supporters pushed down a wall at the Muller Road end of the ground. Rovers' relegation in the summer of 1980/81 spared Chelsea, who narrowly escaped the drop and went on to record league title, and FA Cup triumphs, through the 1990s and into the 21st century.

## ROMAN COINS

COULD Rovers be playing on a crock of Roman gold? In 1875, a group of itinerant labourers laying water-pipes on the site of the *iter xiii* route to Bath, dug up a hoard of Roman coins and carried them away in three bowler hats full to the brim. In February 1934, local resident George Lovell of Fishponds uncovered a Roman coin that dated from the time of Vespasian, Roman Emperor between AD 69 and 79. The Roman roadway *via Julia* ran from Sea Mills to Bath, crossing the area just yards from where Eastville Stadium was to stand almost two millennia later.

## BOBSLEIGH

FOR the game against Chippenham in December 1885, Rovers fielded the interestingly-named centre-half Robert John Sleigh, born in Clifton in the autumn of 1865. Bob Sleigh, an amateur footballer like his team mates, was the fourth child of blacksmith Robert Garrett Sleigh and his wife, Thirza Lush. Three of Thirza's siblings are recorded at West Orchard, as are the banns of marriage for her father's remarriage, to Elizabeth Wates, in November 1874. Bob made just one appearance before working as a tailor's cutter; he and Jane Brice had five daughters before their son William was born in 1900. They lived in a small house in Brighton Terrace, St. George, along with his mother-in-law Harriett Brice.

## SPRINGBOK

THE first Gloucestershire Cup tie in which Rovers played was a 4-1 defeat at Bell Hill against Clifton Association, resplendent in their distinctive 'chocolate and cardinal' shirts. This game in January 1888 featured a goal – Clifton's third – from Charles Wreford-Brown, the first Bristolian to play for England and the man who coined the phrase 'soccer'. The final goal, two minutes from time, was scored by Howard Henry Francis, who was born in Bristol in May 1868. Francis played cricket for Gloucestershire before emigrating to South Africa in 1894 and later played in two Test matches for his adopted country, both against England in 1898/99. He died in Cape Town in January 1936 at the age of 67.

## PENALTY AT BORO

IT is one of those situations you might see in a school playground, yet a professional player slipped whilst taking a penalty in a Third Division match and sent the ball off for a throw-in. This incident happened at Ayresome Park in February 1987, when Rovers conceded a spot kick on the stroke of half-time. Middlesbrough's full-back Brian Laws stepped up to take the kick, but slipped over in the process and was left embarrassed in a crumpled heap, out injured for the rest of the season. After the interval, Stuart Ripley's goal on the hour mark sent Rovers back to the south-west empty-handed. Middlesbrough were promoted back to Division Two at the season's end, three points behind champions AFC Bournemouth.

## THE GAS

PROUDLY known as Gasheads, Rovers supporters owe their sobriquet to the proximity of the Stapleton Road gasworks to the stadium at Eastville. Opened in 1879, the gasworks had its own station on the coal railway that opened on February 10th 1896. The gasworks was bombed by the Luftwaffe during World War II, one bomb totally destroying a house on the corner of Stapleton Road and Sandy Lane, yet carried on to waft gas fumes across the Eastville pitch whilst matches were in progress. Anyone who wishes to view a train used on that line should visit the railway museum in Shildon which houses Merlin. Known at the time as J. Fuller Eberle, the engine was built by the Bristol firm of Pickett and Sons in 1939 and owned by the Bristol United Gas Company until 1968, after which it served in Gloucestershire, north and south Wales, Shropshire and Wiltshire.

## PARRINELLO

TOMMASO Salvatore Parrinello signed for Rovers in August 2006, having previously been at Filton Academy, and looked to be a potential answer to Rovers' quest for a left-back. His parents, Salvatore Parrinello and Graziella Merlino, though of Italian extraction, married in Bristol in March 1988 and young Tom was born in Bristol in November 1989. Just 5ft 3 ins. in height, he played as a substitute in an FA Cup tie in 2007 but never made the league side. Initially loaned to Weston-super-Mare in December 2008 when their full-back Ludovic Quistin was away on international duty with Guadeloupe, Parrinello joined the seaside club on a free transfer in February 2009.

## SEATHERTON'S RECORD

OF all Rovers players, only one who has played in more than one match has a goal-per-game ratio. Step forward Ray Seatherton, born in Tiverton in May 1932, who played in two matches in the spring of 1956, scoring against Lincoln City and Barnsley before a leg injury restricted his progress. He also scored a hat-trick in the opening 25 minutes of a reserve game against Aldershot. Having the astonishing record of 46 goals in only 23 appearances for Minehead prior to joining Rovers in February 1955, he later returned to the Somerset club and then worked for many years as a motor engineer in Tiverton.

# GAS GIRLS

ROVERS' women's side, managed by Tony Ricketts, won promotion to the Premier League in 2002/03, winning their first eight games of the season. The highest win was 13-0 against Barking, with Trudy Williams scoring six goals and Stef Curtis five, whilst a 10-1 win against Forest Green Rovers secured the Gloucestershire County Cup for a fifth consecutive season. The 'Gas Girls' also reached the semi-finals of the FA Cup only to be defeated by a Fulham side that included Rachel McArthur, an England international and granddaughter of Wally McArthur, a Rovers player either side of World War II. Once safely in the Premier League, the side changed its name and, though they continued to play in blue-and-white quarters, were officially separate from the Rovers set-up.

# THE BILLINGHAM RIVET HEATER

INSIDE-left Fred Scotchbrook joined Rovers for the first couple of months of the 1898/99 season and played in eight Birmingham and District League games with the club. One of five children of Frederick Scotchbrook and his wife Susan Coles, a fishmonger, young Fred was born in Whittlesea, Cambridgeshire in the summer of 1882 – his father was caretaker of a steel works – and brought up in Billingham, County Durham, where his father's work had taken the young family. A rivet heater himself, he played five times as a teenage forward with Bolton Wanderers and was in the Bristol St. George side that played Rovers at Eastville on Boxing Day 1898 before a crowd of 14,897. Scotchbrook married Florence Hinchliffe in 1908, coached Stockport County from November 1924 to February 1926, and was manager at Wolves between March 1926 and June 1927. He died in Stockton in the spring of 1936, aged 53.

# TWELFTH MAN

IN the days before allocated substitutes, Rovers would frequently travel with a twelfth man 'just in case'. Such a case was at Stockport County, when Rovers travelled for an FA Cup replay in January 1965 and, with regular inside-right John Brown unable to play during the pre-match warm-up, Alec Munro was hastily called into the side. Rovers lost this game 3-2, Stockport going on to play Division One leaders Liverpool at Anfield in the next round, where they briefly held a lead.

## PIRATE CAP

WHEN Wales played England at Cardiff in March 1906, Jack Lewis became the first player to represent his country whilst on Rovers' books. The inside-right won his only international cap as Wales were defeated 1-0, with Sam Day of Old Malvernians scoring for England. Born in Aberystwyth in the summer of 1882, Lewis scored 30 goals for Rovers in 81 Southern League matches and died in Burton-on-Trent in September 1954.

## EASTER CELEBRATIONS

THE only religious festival to play league football for Rovers was Jamal Easter, who made his debut at Wrexham in October 2006.

## REARRANGED GROUND

THE away game against Millwall in April 1978 was not played in east London, but at Fratton Park, Portsmouth. This was part of a sanction against Millwall following a spate of crowd incidents. Only 3,322 spectators were present for this Division Two fixture and Rovers won 3-1, thanks to strikes from Paul Randall and Steve White, and a Bobby Gould penalty.

## GAS OVERCOME

IN the 1917/18 season, Rovers won 28 out of 37 matches in the Bristol County Combination, scoring 137 goals in the process, yet missed out on the championship to Bristol City. Victories included 13-0 against Great Western Railway, 12-0 over ASC Remounts and 11-0 against a 'Military XI', whilst Bill Weston scored 30 goals in total and Ted Rawlings 21. However, Rovers lost their final two games to their local rivals who pipped them to the title.

## PIRATE INVASION

AN attempt to break a world record was hatched by Rovers fans in the early months of 2010. *The Guinness Book of Records* verified that the largest gathering of pirates in one place was 1,651. Rovers supporters gathered dressed as pirates on Horfield Common prior to the home league fixture with Norwich City in May 2010 in an attempt to break this record.

ROVERS' RECORD SIGNING, PAUL RANDALL, RETURNED TO THE CLUB IN 1978

# QUICK OFF THE MARK

THE fastest goal from the start of a league match involving Rovers was scored after 11 seconds by Leeds United's Bobby Forrest when Rovers played at Elland Road in a Second Division fixture in March 1955. Charlton Athletic's Sam Lawrie scored against Rovers in the FA Cup in January 1959 after just 19 seconds. The fastest scored in Rovers' favour was scored by Keith Curle, who was later sent off, in the 1-1 draw with Millwall in April 1983. It was timed at 25 seconds, one second faster than that scored by Marcus Stewart against Hull City in January 1996, and two seconds faster than Marcus Bignot in the local derby against Bristol City in December 2000. Ken Ronaldson scored against Southport in September 1967 after 28 seconds. In other matches, Dai Ward scored after seven seconds in a Gloucestershire Cup tie against Bristol City in May 1959, Vic Lambden scored after eight seconds in the FA Cup against Aldershot in January 1951 and Jim Hyam scored in the Southern League against Southampton in December 1919 after 12 seconds. The first time Rovers scored a first-minute goal was Fred Channing's strike in the 1-0 home win over Southville in January 1889.

# YOUNGEST GOALSCORING PIRATES

RONNIE Dix is the youngest player to score in the league for any club in Football League history, one of only four 15-year-olds to score, as well as the fourth-youngest player to have appeared in the league. Dix scored Rovers' second goal in a 3-0 home win against Norwich City in March 1928, with a rasping drive after 70 minutes. Steve Williams scored only once in league football, though he was to win three consecutive Welsh League titles with Barry Town before his untimely death in December 1999, aged just 36.

1. Ronnie Dix ........... b. 05/09/12 .... sc. 03/03/28 ........ 15 years 180 days
2. Steve Williams ..... b. 27/04/63 .... sc. 19/12/80 ........ 17 years 208 days
3. Nathan Ellington b. 02/07/81 .... sc. 06/03/99 ........ 17 years 247 days
4. Keith Curle .......... b. 14/11/63 .... sc. 29/08/81 ........ 17 years 288 days
5. Neil Slatter ........... b. 30/05/64 .... sc. 17/04/82 ........ 17 years 322 days

## 1889 EASTVILLE FLOODS

THE perennial issue of flooding pervades Rovers' story, the old ground at Eastville being close to the River Frome and even the lyrics of the club anthem Goodnight Irene hint at the constant threat of drowning. In March 1889, serious flooding blocked off much of Eastville, some 200 acres being underwater as the snow thawed leaving Sevier Street impassable. Walter Clarke rescued 40 passengers from a tramcar stuck in the floods but, as he rowed home, the current took him and he had to jump overboard himself and swim. George Vince, who ran the Railway Inn in Stapleton Road, rescued a further 40 passengers from a different tramcar. A Mr Chenhall, who ran an engineering works in Wolseley Road, Eastville, constructing steam launches, lived with his family for several days above his workshop, where they could hear the furniture in seven feet of water bumping against the ceiling. A Floods Relief Fund had, within four weeks, raised the grand sum of £11,700. The danger of flooding did not disappear until extensive work was carried out through the 1960s.

## LOCAL HACKS

A NUMBER of journalists have covered Rovers matches for the local press down the years. Early writers wrote under pseudonyms, such as 'Scribe' Tom Smith, 'Half Back' Slater Stone and 'The Traveller' Bill Pinnell, who retired on New Year's Eve 1956 and died in January 1977 at the age of 89. John Coe reported on Rovers games for the *Bristol Evening Post* from 1938 to 1961, before he was replaced by Robin Perry, whose first game was the match against Liverpool in August 1961. His counterpart at the *Bristol Evening World* was Pat Kavanagh from 1946 to 1962. Since the early 1960s, a succession of journalists have reported Rovers' progress through radio, television, newspapers and the Internet.

## BOTH AT HOME

IN May 1947, both Rovers and City played at home on the same day, in the sort of situation that modern strategic and logistical preparations would not allow to happen. Rovers held Ipswich Town to a 1-1 draw at Eastville before a crowd of 10,459 with Fred Leamon scoring the goal, before City drew 1-1 with Queens Park Rangers in a 6.30pm kick-off.

## PLAYER OF THE YEAR

DOUG Hillard was the first Rovers Player of the Year, winning in 1962/63. He won again in 1965/66; Ray Mabbutt and Joe Davis having been named as players of the season in the intervening years.

## BERT WILLIAMS

BERT Williams, who died in September 1929, was credited as the man who 'discovered' Wally Hammond, Rovers player and England cricketer, just as a tea lady 'discovered' the future England goalkeeper Nigel Martyn. Bert Williams was Rovers' groundsman from 1918 to 1920 and club trainer from then until 1962. He died, aged 80, in Bristol in March 1982.

## X MARKS THE SPOT

RECENTLY, Lee Zabek, Bobby Zamora, James Quinn, Rob Quinn and Anwar U'ddin have represented Rovers in league football, leaving X as the only letter with which no Rovers player's surname has started.

## TOM WALKER

A NOTABLE figure amongst many working behind the club's scenes for many years was Thomas George Walker. Born in August 1864, he was a club director for 11 years and, from 1927, took on the role of chairman of the Supporters' Club. Tom Walker died in Bristol in February 1933 aged 68.

## OFF TO SCOTLAND

IN the summers of 1982 and 1983, Rovers embarked on three-game tours of Scotland. In August 1982, a 2-1 win at Partick Thistle and a 3-2 victory at Falkirk were followed by a resounding 4-1 thumping of Ayr United, with Paul Randall twice and Errington Kelly and Mike Barrett all scoring before half-time. Twelve months later, Rovers drew 1-1 with Airdrieonians and won 3-0 at Hamilton Academical, where Aiden McCaffrey, Ian Holloway and Brian Williams all scored in a six-minute burst after half-time, before David Williams' 78th-minute strike earned a 2-1 win at Kilmarnock's Rugby Park.